FINALE

FOR COMPOSERS

An Illustrated Guide
to Finale®

Keith A. Bajura

20TH ANNIVERSARY EDITION

An Illustrated Guide to Finale®

Finale® for Composers

20th Anniversary Edition

Written by Keith Bajura

Edited by Amy Stabenow

Phoebus Apollo Music

704 Decatur Avenue
Pittsburgh, PA 15221
(412) 271-2849
(412) 727-1282 Fax

Find us on the World Wide Web at: www.phoebusapollo.com

To report errors, please send a note to errata@phoebusapollo.com

ISBN: 978-0-9753953-2-5

0 9 8 7 6 5 4 3 2 1

Printed in the United States of America

Finale for Composers
An Illustrated Guide to Finale
20th Anniversary Edition
By Keith A. Bajura

Table of Contents

Much has changed with Finale® since my first edition of *Finale for Composers*. It has taken me several years to write this second edition. With a new version of Finale every year, it was difficult to stay current. In a nutshell, there are a now fewer tools, but the tools that remain are more powerful and perform multiple functions. No longer do you have to use two or three tools to accomplish a common task. You are able do the same thing more quickly and more efficiently with the same tool. You may even think that the tools have become "smarter." Almost all tools now have contextual menus which change based on what is selected. You access these menus by right clicking if you have a two-button mouse or by option-clicking on the Mac. Commonly used functions such as changing the key or time signature can be easily accomplished with one right click on the mouse.

The other major upgrade in Finale is the addition of the Garritan Instruments. No longer are you stuck with the wimpy QuickTime sounds nor do you have to connect to an external synthesizer. With each new edition, the playback has become better and better.

After countless hours of using Finale, hundreds of phone calls from musicians asking for help in Finale, and numerous lectures in the classroom teaching Finale at Carnegie Mellon University, I finally took the advice of my many colleagues, clients, friends, and students and set out to write a book on Finale. But not just any book... a book that focuses on Finale as a tool for composers. In order to get the most out of this book, I would suggest that you have at least a basic knowledge of the workings of Finale. While I will cover the more elusive features, which many users may not know, I occasionally have omitted some of the more basic skills. These skills can be easily learned from the user guide.

The majority of the students at Carnegie Mellon University who took my Finale class were composers. I have seen firsthand that composers have different needs for Finale than other users do. They want to quickly and easily work with contemporary notation using Finale. They want to know how to make their parts look professionally printed with the least amount of time and effort, usually waiting to the last minute to print them. (Remember, they are students). They want their MIDI playback to be accurate and as real sounding as possible. But, the biggest difference by far is that they ask questions... a lot of questions. By far the most common question is: "Can Finale do this?" The answer 99.9% of the time is yes! Knowing how to get Finale to do it is the real question. This book is my answer to that question. Hopefully, composers, copyists, arrangers, and anyone else who would like to learn more of what makes Finale the best program for professional and contemporary music will find learning the more advanced areas of Finale quick and complete.

It is hard to believe that Finale is twenty years old. I can still remember the day that changed my entire life. I was standing in the downtown branch of the *Pittsburgh Computer Store* (in Pittsburgh, PA of course), purchasing version 1.0 of Finale back in 1988. I was a sophomore at Carnegie Mellon University majoring in music composition. I had been using some other very primitive notation program at that time and was happy to find something better. I can't remember the price I paid. It was either $595 or $494 or maybe even $295. I do know was that it was on sale and it was "going fast" so I had to jump in my car, speed downtown and double park just to get it before it sold out. I still have the original box with the manuals and video. When Finale debuted, people were more impressed with the box than with the program. The box and manuals, when compared to today's standard, seem extravagant, and I believed they were rumored to cost over $100. The box, which is actually one and a half boxes that nest inside each other, is a hard shiny cardboard containing a very impressive canvas three ring binder. The binder in turn contained a video as well as three spiral bound manuals—a User's Guide, Reference Manual, and Power User's Guide. And, the whole package was only available for Mac. I am sure that it must be a collector's item now, but I promised myself it will never find itself listed on eBay as so many of my other "treasures" have.

In the beginning, Coda created Finale and it was good. Well okay, it was good but very few people realized its potential at first. The interface was clunky with a different type of click needed to accomplish various tasks—command-click for this, shift-click for that, and option-click for who remembers what. And the learning curve was steeper than Mount Everest, making it all the more appealing to me. I love a challenge and no program, no matter how difficult, was going to get the better of me. So after a few weeks of fooling around with the thing, reading all of the manuals, watching the video, and hours of trial and error, I became a Finale aficionado. From that point on, I jumped right in for every upgrade they offered. I even switched between Mac and PC a few times just for good measure and used it on everything from my old Mac SE/30 to my current 2.4 GHz Quad Core 2 Duo running Vista Ultimate 64 bit.

I have used Finale to print everything from simple rhythmic patterns for Eurhythmics exercises to full-blown Symphonies and Operas that were performed by professional orchestras as well as everything in between. Finale has helped me when I needed to quickly arrange a hymn for my limited voice church choir, and has brought me enough clients to start a side business as a music copyist. You may have laughed earlier when I said that Finale has changed my life, but I believe that Finale has made all of these things possible for me. I would be at a very different place in my life if it were not for Finale. Now I would like to share my success in using Finale with you in this book so you can see what it can do for you.

Tools covered in this chapter are listed below:

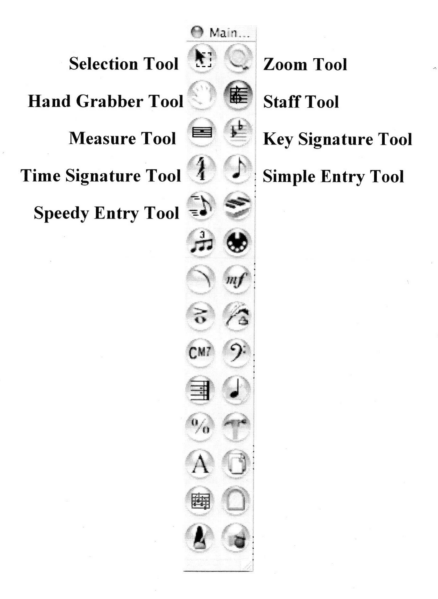

Selection Tool	**Zoom Tool**
Hand Grabber Tool	**Staff Tool**
Measure Tool	**Key Signature Tool**
Time Signature Tool	**Simple Entry Tool**
Speedy Entry Tool	

Finale is based around the idea that the majority of tasks you need to perform can be easily accomplished by clicking on a tool found on Finale's Main Tool Palette. Below is that palette. All the tools are labeled. Some may appear confusing at first. For example, do you change the clef with the tool that looks like the Bass Clef or the one with the Treble Clef and Staff? Others such as the Time Signature and Key Signature tools are very clear in what they do. If you recently upgraded from an older version of Finale, you might be wondering "where is the little red truck (Mass Mover) tool?" Other tools are just strange and almost fanciful. The mirror and the feather pen for example… have any idea of what they do? Read on to find out.

The Main Tool Palette:

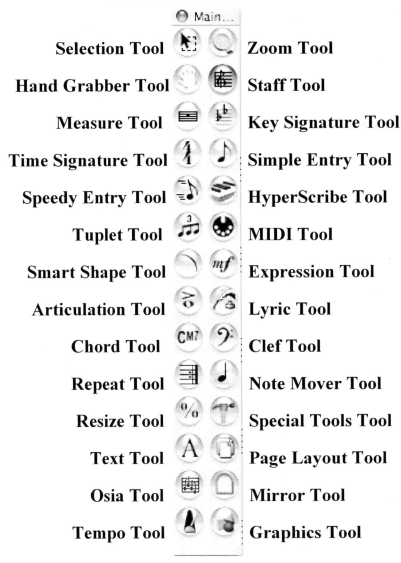

Selection Tool	Zoom Tool
Hand Grabber Tool	Staff Tool
Measure Tool	Key Signature Tool
Time Signature Tool	Simple Entry Tool
Speedy Entry Tool	HyperScribe Tool
Tuplet Tool	MIDI Tool
Smart Shape Tool	Expression Tool
Articulation Tool	Lyric Tool
Chord Tool	Clef Tool
Repeat Tool	Note Mover Tool
Resize Tool	Special Tools Tool
Text Tool	Page Layout Tool
Osia Tool	Mirror Tool
Tempo Tool	Graphics Tool

If you have previously used Finale, you may be tempted to skip over these first few chapters. I would ask that you resist that urge. Even students in my Finale classes who consider themselves to be very familiar with Finale, inevitably learned something new when covering the most basic material.

There being so many different tools on the Main Tool Palette, you might think "Where should I start?" I have always taken the approach when starting to learn Finale as if I were going to write a piece of music. Pretend there is a blank piece of manuscript paper before you and your pencil in hand. What's the first thing you need to do? I think most people would agree that you need to draw three things on the page: the clef, the key signature, and the time signature. Those will be the three tools we will look at first. These three tools are also among the easiest tools to use and have fewer options than the other tools. They provide a good place for us to start:

Clef Tool

The Clef Tool serves one and only one purpose—to change the clefs used in your music. It has two main options: You can change the clef at the start of a measure and the music will be notated in the new clef after the barline. Or, you can place one or several clefs in the middle of the measure and the music will be notated using the new clef directly following the clef change. This is called a moveable mid-measure clef change. See the following example of both clef changes.

Finale Terminology:

Moveable Mid-Measure Clef: A clef created with the Clef Tool that can be positioned anywhere within the measure. Notes following the Moveable Mid-Measure Clef are notated using the clef. Notes before the Moveable Mid-Measure Clef, are notated using the previous clef. You can have more than one Moveable Mid-Measure Clef in each measure. To delete a Moveable Mid-Measure Clef, click on the measure containing it then click on its corresponding handle and press Delete on your keyboard.

Handle: Small boxes that are used throughout Finale to select, position, edit or delete various items. Depending on which tool is selected, these boxes appear by certain items that can then be modified. When a handle is selected, the small box turns black. Many tools use handles to delete or cancel a function when you press Delete on your computer keyboard when a handle is selected.

Examples of handles.

BMCC   BMCC   BMCC   MMCC   BMCC   MMCC   MMCC   MMCC

BMCC= Beginning of Measure Clef Change
MMCC= Moveable Mid-Measure Clef Change

To change the clef:
- Select the Clef Tool
- Click on the measure where you want the new clef to be used or on the measure where you would like to create a moveable mid-measure clef.
- Select the clef you would like to use.
- **NEW for 2009:** Create a mid-measure clef by dragging the selection around the note(s) you want to have in the new clef.
- Specify the measure region you want the new clef to span.
- Click OK

Show Clef Options:
You can also use the Clef Tool to show or hide clefs. Under the Show Clef options, select "Never" to hide a clef or "Always" to show a clef for a certain measure. The Clef Size ___% box also allows you to scale a clef either larger or smaller.

Measure Range Options:
Under the Measure Range options, you can either specify a range of measures in which to use the new clef, or you can specify to use the new clef on a certain measure through the end of the piece. When using this option, all other clef changes in this region will be deleted and all music will use the clef you specify. Newer versions of Finale also have a third option that allows you to specify a starting measure and the clef change affecting the music from that point up until the next clef change. Unlike using the "Through the End of Piece" option, this option will not change any previously existing clef changes.

Special Mouse Clicks

- Drag a mid-measure clef handle across the left barline to convert it to a regular clef change (where the clef appears to the left of the barline).
- Double-click a mid-measure clef handle; on the second click, hold the mouse button down and drag the handle right or left to change the clef (from a bass clef to a treble clef, for example). As you drag the clef horizontally, it cycles through its eighteen available clefs.
- Option-click a mid-measure clef handle, or control-click the handle and select Edit Clef Definition from the contextual menu to display the mid-measure Clef dialog box, where you can change the clef, specify its positioning, or turn it back into a single clef (one that appears just before the first barline of the measure and can't be moved).
- Double-click a highlighted region of measures to open the Clef Selection dialog box where you can change the clef for all measures in the region.

Key Signature Tool

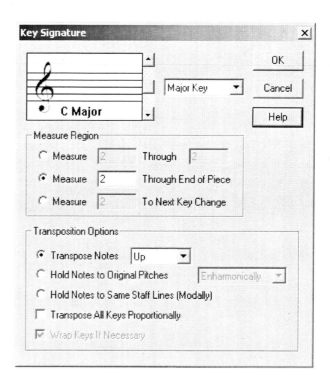

The Key Signature Tool is also straightforward in what it can do. It can change the Key Signature in your piece and has several options on how to deal with any existing music that would be affected by the key change. It functions much like the Clef Tool—double-click on the measure in which you want to change the key and make any changes to the Key Signature window. The dropdown menu allows specifying a major, minor, or non-standard key signature. While you might realize that the key signature for C Major is the same as A Minor, Finale uses the major or minor mode setting to help notate such things as accidentals and chords in your piece. Take the extra time and set this correctly if you are working in a tonal piece and you will save time later correcting wrong accidentals. Non-standard key signature setting allows you to create your own key signature using more than seven sharps or flats. Or, you can depart from the circle of fifths all together and create a key signature with any number of sharps and/or flats. See chapter 14 for more information.

To change the clef:

- Select the Key Signature Tool
- Double-click on the measure where you want the new key signature to start. You can also drag a selection around the measures that you would like to use in the new key. This will automatically fill in the starting and ending measure for the Measure Region setting.
- Set the Major or Minor Key from the drop-down menu.
- Use the scroll bar to cycle through the key signatures until you find the one you want. Scrolling up removes flats and adds sharps; scrolling down removes sharps and adds flats.
- Specify the measure region that you want the new key signature to span.
- Specify any Transposition Options.
- Click OK.

Measure Range Options:

Under the Measure Range options, you can either specify a range of measures that you want to use the new key signature, or you can specify to use the new key signature on a certain measure through the end of the piece. When using this option, all other key changes in this region will be deleted and all music will use the key signature you specify. Newer versions of Finale also have a third option that allows you to specify a starting measure. The key change will affect the music from that point to the next key change. Unlike using the "Through the End of Piece" option, this option will not change any previously existing key changes.

Transposition Options:

When changing the key of existing music, Finale needs to know what to do with the pitches of that music. There are three options you have when telling Finale how to treat the existing music:

- Transpose the notes (up or down). The existing notes will be transposed from the old key to the new key either higher or lower according to the option you choose. This is an easy way to take existing music and transpose it into a new key—just change the key signature.
- Hold Notes to Original Pitches (Enharmonically/Chromatically). This can be thought of as the "no transposition" option. Notes are kept at their exact pitches. However, if you set the "Enharmonically" option, notes will change to their enharmonic equivalent if appropriate. For example, a C-sharp will change to a D-flat if the new key contains it. If you want the pitches to remain absolutely the same, use the chromatic option and no changes will occur (except added naturals where needed).
- Hold Notes to Same Staff Lines (Modally). The notes will remain on the same line or space but will be affected by the new key signature, but without having accidentals added. For example, an F-natural in the key of C will be changed in an F-sharp in the key of G because of the key signature, but no new accidental will be added.

See the following examples of all three transpose options:

Other Options:

- Transpose All Keys Proportionally: Determines whether to shift subsequent key changes within the measures you selected so that they maintain their relationship to the measure you clicked. For example, you have an existing key change that goes from G major to D major (up a fifth) later in your piece. You then change the starting key of G major to A major (up a second). If the "Transpose All Keys Proportionally" is selected, the subsequent key change to D major will transpose proportionally up a second to E major. If this option is not checked, all key changes are cleared and everything is changed into the key you select. In this example, the entire selection would be notated in A major.

- Wrap Keys If Necessary: Determines whether key signatures will "wrap around" during proportional key changes preventing keys with more than seven sharps or flats from occurring. This option is only available when "Transpose All Keys Proportionally" is checked and turns on automatically at that time. This option prevents keys like G-sharp major from occurring and will change them into enharmonic keys such as A-flat major. If not checked, key signatures with double flats or double sharps may occur.

 **Special Mouse Clicks**

- Drag-enclose an area to select a region of music for Metatools, or for the Key Signature dialog box to affect.

Time Signature Tool

The third in our trio of new tools, the Time Signature Tool also functions similarly to the other two we have looked at so far. This tool is used to change the time signature throughout your piece. It can also be used to create composite time signatures 3+2/8 or to display a different time signature other than what the music is actually using.

To change the time signature:

• Select the Time Signature Tool

• Double-click on the measure where you want the new key signature to start. You can also drag a selection around the measures you would like to incorporate the new time signature. This will automatically fill in the starting and ending measure for the Measure Region setting.

• Use the upper scroll bar to increase or decrease the number of beats per measure.

• Use the lower scroll bar to increase or decrease the length of the beat. (See chart below). Your music will be beamed ac-cording to the time signature you set. Make sure you set it properly.

• Specify the measure region you want the new time signature to span.

• Click OK.

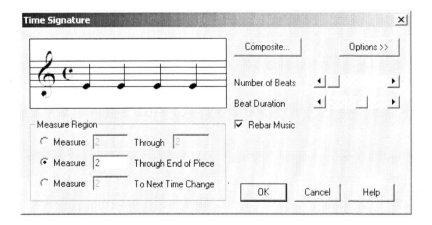

The following chart shows the list of the length of the beat options

Beat Duration Scroll Bar Position			Meter represented by 2, 3, and 4 beats to a measure.
All the way to the left =	♪ (thirty-second)	Thirty-second note	2/32, 3/32, 4/32
	♪. (dotted thirty-second)	Dotted thirty-second note	6/64, 9/64, 12/64
	♪ (sixteenth)	Sixteenth Note	2/16, 3/16, 4/16
	♪. (dotted sixteenth)	Dotted Sixteenth Note	6/32, 9/32, 12/32
	♪ (eighth)	Eighth Note	2/8, 3/8, 4/8
	♪. (dotted eighth)	Dotted Eight Note	6/16, 9/16, 12/16
	♩ (quarter)	Quarter Note	2/4, 3/4, 4/4
	♩. (dotted quarter)	Dotted Quarter Note	6/8, 9/8, 12/8
	𝅗𝅥 (half)	Half Note	2/2, 3/2, 4/2
	𝅗𝅥. (dotted half)	Dotted Half Note	6/4, 9/4, 12/4
All the way to the right=	𝅝 (whole)	Whole Note	2/1, 3/1, 4/1

Important:

Often, there is more than one way to display a time signature. Even though time signatures look the same on the screen, they are not, in fact, exactly the same. Time signatures control such things as beaming and note placement. Be sure that you are using the correct signature for your purpose. If you don't, you will have extra unnecessary editing to do.

To create a time signature properly, you must think in terms of how many beats there are in each measure and more importantly, the length of each beat. For example, 4/4 is four beats per measure where the beat is based on a quarter note. 6/8 on the other hand, is two beats per measure where the dotted quarter note gets the beat. One pitfall to avoid is setting up 6/8 with six as the number of beats and a beat duration of the eighth note. Just as shown in the time signature window, your measures will consist of six unbeamed eighth notes.

The following examples further illustrate this point:

Number of beats: 6
Duration of beat: Eighth Note

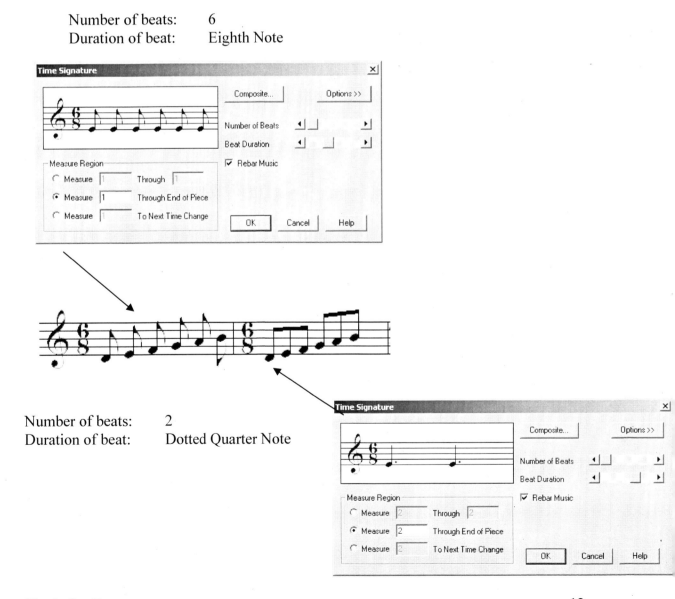

Number of beats: 2
Duration of beat: Dotted Quarter Note

Composite Time Signatures:

In Finale, you also have the ability to create very complex composite time signatures such as 2+2+3/8 or 2.75/4. While these types of time signatures are often found in contemporary music, they are also very useful for beaming purposes. For example, you can define a composite time signature of 3+2/8 so that all music will be beamed in a group of three and then a group of two in every measure. You can also use the "Use a Different Time Signature for Display" (see below) to have a displayed time signature of 5/8 instead of the 3+2/8 which Finale is using to beam the notes.

Click the Composite button in the main Time Signature window to define a composite time signature:

In the Composite Time Signature window, there are five boxes in which you can enter values for Beat Groups (the upper portion of the time signature) and five corresponding boxes to enter Beat Durations for each of the five Beat Groups the lower portion of the time signature).

When defining Beat Durations, use "4" for quarter note, "8" for eighth note, "2" for half note, etc. Other numbers such as "3", "5", "6", "7", etc. will be rounded up to the next valid number.

In order to specify triple meters in the Composite Time Signature window such as 6/8 or 9/8 where the Beat Duration is actually a dotted quarter note, you must use EDU's for the Beat Duration.

Finale Terminology:

EDU: *Enigma Durational Unit.* There are 1024 EDU's per quarter note. Therefore, by way of example, an eighth note would have 512 and a dotted quarter note would have 1536 EDU's. This is very similar to the idea of a "tick" when working with MIDI. However, there are always 1024 EDU's in a quarter note. This value can never change as it can with MIDI Ticks.

By clicking the "Use EDU's for Beat Duration," you are now able to specify dotted notes.

Notice how 6/8 is defined by using 2 beat groups of 1536 EDU's (which corresponds to a dotted quarter note). The 3/4 is defined as 3 beat groups of 1024 EDU's or 3 quarter notes.

Note: Once you click the "Use EDU's" button, all Beat Durations must be entered in EDU's.

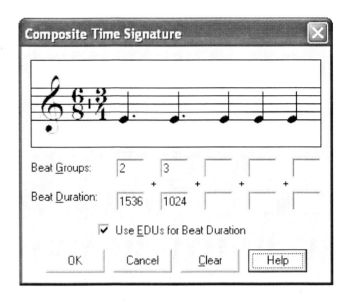

You also can enter beat groups within a beat group such as 3+2/8 as shown here. This is very useful for beaming purposes. If you would like to use a different time signature for the music, click options then "Use a Different Time Signature for Display" (see below).

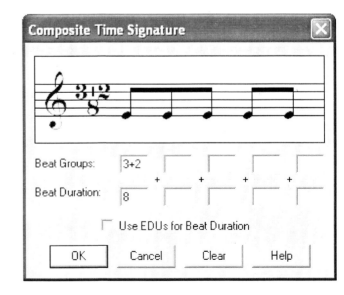

You can also use decimals as part of the Beat Group. Here it is defined as 3.75/4:

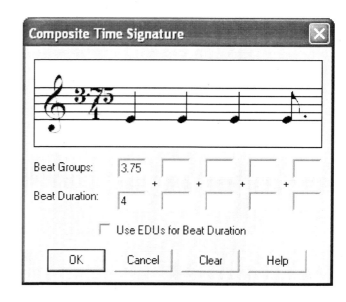

If you change your mind and want to revert to a non-composite time Signature, click the "Clear" button. You will be taken back to the regular time signature window.

Other Options:

Rebar: If you are changing the time signature for existing music, you usually would want the music to be rebarred so that there are the proper number of beats in each measure. Checking this option does just that: repositions the barlines to reflect the new time signature adding barlines where needed and moving notes to previous or subsequent measures. If you do not select this option, the music stays barred the way it was before you changed the time signature and probably has either too few or too many beats in some bars.

Use a Different Time Signature for Display: Allows you to create a second time signature exactly like you did the first one that will be displayed in the music, while at first glance this might seem like a useless option. Why would anyone ever want to display a time signature other than the one in which the music is notated in? This option allows you to beam your music according to one time signature (the first one you set with the Time Signature Tool) but have a completely different time signature displayed in the music. As with the actual time signature, this "display only" time signature can also be a composite time signature.

Abbreviate: This controls whether to display either 4/4 or **C** for common time and 2/2 or **C** for cut time. This option is also available under Document Settings/Time Signature Options. In earlier versions of the program, you only have the option to change this display under Document Settings/Time Signature Options.

 **Special Mouse Clicks**

- Drag-enclose an area to select a region of music for Metatools, or for the Time Signature dialog box to affect.

Navigational Tools

Finale also offers three tools for positioning your music on the page and making the music easier to read by enlarging or reducing it.

 Hand Grabber Tool: Lets you position the music that is currently showing on your screen. Click and drag the music up or down, left or right to adjust what is currently viewable on the screen. Note: this does not change the measure your are viewing; i.e. you cannot scroll through your document with the Hand Grabber Tool.

 Special Mouse Clicks

- While using any other tool, press the right mouse button to switch temporarily to the Hand Grabber Tool. Drag in the score to make a display adjustment without having to move the mouse to the Navigational Tools Palette

Zoom Tool: Enlarges/magnifies or shrinks/reduces the music on the screen. With the tool selected, click anywhere to zoom in to twice the current size. Option-click on Macs or Ctrl-click on PCs to reduce by one half the current size. Note: this does not actually enlarge or reduce the size of your printed music. (See the Resize Tool in Chapter 6 to perform that action.)

Special Mouse Clicks

- Click the music or press Command + (plus) to zoom in incrementally.
- Option-click the music or press Command -(minus) to zoom out incrementally.
- In Page View, drag diagonally across a region of music to enlarge it just enough to fill your screen.
- While using any other tool, command-shift–click the screen to zoom in, even though the Zoom Tool isn't selected. Command-option-shift–click to zoom out.

Selection Tool:

The Selection Tool is Finale's universal editing tool. It can be used to select, move, delete, copy, paste, or otherwise edit any region of measures and virtually any individual item in the score.

Click on a marking to select it, such as a lyric, slur or articulation. Once selected, you can move, nudge, edit or delete it. For more advanced editing, double-click to switch to the appropriate tool. The Selection Tool works on Measures (Measure Tool/Edit Menu/Utilities Menu), Notes & Rests (Simple Entry), Smart Shapes, Expressions, Articulations, Repeats, Lyrics, Chords & Fretboards, Text Blocks, Graphics, Brackets, Measure Numbers, Tuplets, Key and Time Signatures, Clefs, Ossia's, Staff and Group Names.

This tool is also used to select regions of your score (from a single note to the entire score) in order to edit all the selected music at once. For example, you can change any selected measures' spacing, measure widths, layer assignments, stem directions, beaming patterns, and so on. You can also rebeam, rebar, transpose, or apply articulations to every note in any selected region.

You can use this tool to copy music from one place to another—even from one Finale document to another. You can also use this tool for erasing selected musical elements from a region—such as articulations, chord symbols, lyrics, expressions, MIDI controller data, and so on—without disturbing the other existing elements of the music in that region.

 Special Mouse Clicks
- Press Command-shift-A or the Esc key to switch to the Selection Tool.
- Click an item to select it. If two items overlap, click again to cycle through the overlapping items.
- Drag a selected item to move it.
- Select an item then use the arrow keys to nudge an item.
- Select an item and hit clear to restore default positioning.
- Click and press delete, or control-click the handle and select Delete from the contextual menu to remove an item.
- Double-click an item or press return with an item selected to select the item with the appropriate tool.

Entering Notes Using the Simple Entry Tool

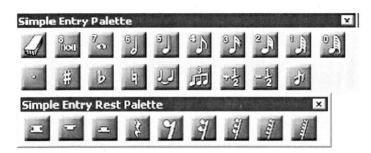

- The simplest way to put notes on the staff.
- Click on the note duration you want and then click the note on the staff.
- Use the eraser to delete notes.
- **Hold down numbers 0 through 8 to automatically select that note value.**
- Options:
    - **Check for Extra Notes.**
    - **Create New Measures.**
    - **Fill with Rests at End of Measure-** Finale adds rests to complete the measure.
    - **Launch Layer Mid-Measure**
    - **Playback-** every time you enter or change the pitch of a note, you will hear the new pitch
    - **Select Notes on Entry-** When this item is selected, you can immediately use keyboard shortcuts to modify the note that was just entered.
    - **Select Tablature Notes on Entry-** When this item is selected, you can immediately use keyboard shortcuts to modify the last fret number added to a tablature staff.
    - **Simple Edit Commands submenu-** Lists the Other Simple Edit commands and their keyboard shortcuts.

Entering Notes or Rests:
- **Press numpad 1-8 (or Command-Option-Shift 1-8),** then click on the staff to enter a 64th note through double whole note. Select the duration and then press "." (period) to specify a dotted note.
- **Press 9 and then numpad 1-8** (or Command-Option-Shift 1-8), and then click on the staff to enter a tuplet based on the duration.
- **Press T, then numpad 1-8 (or Command-Option-Shift 1-8),** and then click on the staff to enter a tied note.
- **Click the Eraser Tool** then click a note, rest, accidental, tuplet, tie or dot to erase it.

- With a note selected, **press Enter to activate the Simple Entry Caret.**

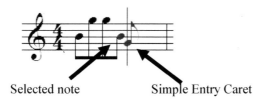

Selected note   Simple Entry Caret

- **Press the up arrow key** to move the caret up diatonically, or the **down arrow key** to move the caret down diatonically.
- **Hold down Shift and press the up arrow key** to move the caret up an octave, or the **down arrow key** to move the caret down an octave.
- **With the caret active, press numpad 1-8 (or Command-Option-Shift 1-8)** to select a duration, 64th note through double-whole note, for the next note entered. Select the duration and then press "." (period) to specify a dotted note.
- **With the caret active, press Enter** to enter a note at the pitch specified on the staff of the rhythmic duration chosen in the Simple Entry Palette. (Notes entered with the caret are selected automatically.)
- **With the caret active, press a letter key A-G** to enter a note of that pitch. Finale enters the note within the range of a fourth higher or lower than the pitch specified on the caret.
- **With the caret active, press 0 to enter a rest** on the staff of the rhythmic duration chosen in the Simple Entry Palette.
- **With a note selected, hold down Shift and press a letter key A-G** to add a note of that pitch to the selected note. Finale adds the note within the range of a fourth higher or lower than the pitch specified on the caret. The added note is selected.
- After entering a note with the caret, **hold down Command and press Enter** to add a note to the previous entry at the pitch specified by the caret.
- **Press a number key 1-8 (on the QWERTY keyboard)** to add a note of that interval (unison through octave) above the selected note. The added note is selected.
- **Hold down Shift and Command and press 9 on the QWERTY** keyboard to add a ninth above the selected note. The added note is selected.
- **Hold down Shift and press a number key 1-9 on the QWERTY keyboard** to add a note of that interval (unison through ninth) below the selected note. The added note is selected.
- With the caret active, **play a note or chord on a MIDI keyboard** to enter pitch(es) of the chosen duration.
- **Press the Escape key to hide the Simple Entry Caret.**

Accidentals

Key Combination	Note Selected	Note Not Selected
=	♯	Selects the Sharp Tool
-	♭	Selects the Flat Tool
N	(♮)	Selects the Natural Tool
[shift] – (minus)	♭♭	N/A
[shift] =	𝄪	N/A
[numpad] – (minus)	Lowered ½ step	Selects the Half Step Down Tool
[numpad] + (plus)	Raised ½ step	Selects the Half Step Up Tool
[command][shift] – (minus)	Show/Hide Accidental	N/A
P	Show/Hide Parenthesized Accidental (♯) (♭)etc.	N/A

Beams, Stems and Ties

- **Select a note then press "T"** to tie the selected note to the next note.
- **Press Shift "T"** to tie the selected note to the previous note.
- **Press "/"** to break or join the beam on the selected note.
- **Press Shift "/"** to restore default beaming.
- **Press Option "/"** to create a flat beam.
- **Press "L"** to flip the stem of the selected note.
- **Press Shift "L"** to restore the default stem direction.

Changing the Time, Key, or Clef in Simple Entry

- **Select a note, press Option-K** and press a key signature Metatool key to change the key signature or click Select to open the Key Signature dialog box where you can specify the new key.
- **Select a note, press Option-T** and press a time signature Metatool key to change the time signature or click Select ore press Enter to open the Time Signature dialog box where you can specify the new meter. The key change appears at the current measure.
- **Select a note, press Option-C** and press a clef Metatool key to change the clef or click Select or press Enter to open the Change Clef dialog box dialog box where you can specify the placement and clef type for the clef change.

Exercise 1.1
Enter the following music **using only the Simple Entry Tool:**

Speedy Entry Tool WITHOUT MIDI

Speedy Entry Options:

- Use with or without MIDI Keyboard.
- Playback During Drag- Plays the pitches when you drag a note.
- Jump to Next Measure.
- Create new measures.
- Check Beaming (automatically beams notes together according to the time signature).
- Check Accidentals (automatically puts in the correct accidentals).
- Check for Extra Notes.
- Use Five Line Staff (uses a five line staff even though the staff uses something different).
- Edit TAB As Standard Notation- displays notes in tablature staves instead of fret numbers while in a Speedy editing frame. After exiting the editing frame, Finale will display the fret numbers.
- Auto Freeze Accidentals (makes sure that the other accidentals don't change when you show or hide accidentals using the "*" key.
- Insert Notes or Rests.

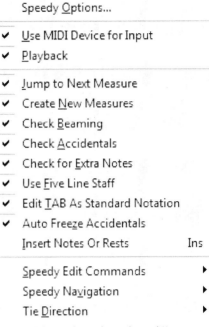

Use the numeric keypad to enter note values:

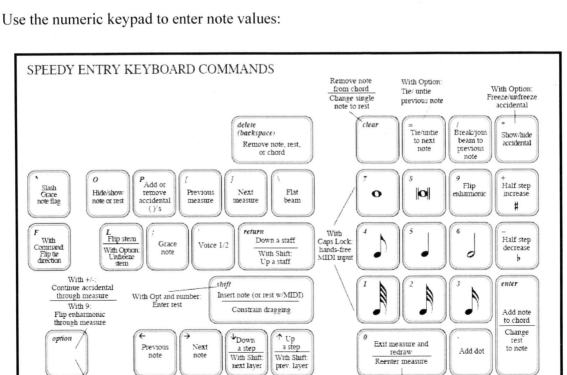

Speedy Entry Command Shortcuts:

Add Note	enter
Delete Note	backspace
Delete Entry	delete
Show/Hide Entry	O
Raise Half Step	+
Lower Half Step	-
Raise Half Step (Entire Measure)	Ctrl++
Lower Half Step (Entire Measure)	Ctrl+-
Show/Hide Accidental	*
Freeze/Unfreeze Accidental	Ctrl+*
Enharmonic	9
Enharmonic (Entire Measure)	Ctrl+9
Add/Remove Accidental Parentheses	P
Flip Stem Direction	L
Set Stem Direction to Automatic	Ctrl+L
Break/Join Beam	/
Flat Beam	\
Tie/Untie to Next Note	=
Tie/Untie to Prev Note	Ctrl+=
Add Dot	.
Grace Note	;
Slash Grace Note	`
Freeze/Float Rest	*

Speedy Entry Navigational Shortcut:

Previous Measure	[, Shift+left arrow
Next Measure	], Shift+right arrow
Next Layer	"
Change Voice	'
Up Staff	Shift+up arrow
Down Staff	Shift+down arrow
Start of Measure	Ctrl+left arrow
End of Measure	Ctrl+right arrow
Previous Note	left arrow
Next Note	right arrow
Up Step	up arrow
Down Step	down arrow

Tie Direction Shortcuts:

Flip	Ctrl+F
Automatic	Ctrl+Shift+F
Over	
Under	

 Special Mouse Clicks

- Ctrl-click any measure containing entries to display the Edit Frame dialog box, which contains dozens of very technical parameters for each note in the measure.
- Press Ctrl-number to tell Finale that the next notes you enter are part of a tuplet (triplet, quintuplet, and so on). Press Ctrl-2 through Ctrl-8 to signify tuplets from duplets to octuplets, respectively. If you press Ctrl-1, the Tuplet Definition dialog box appears where you can enter more complex tuplet groupings.
- Press Caps Lock before pressing a rhythmic-value key to tell Finale that you're about to enter a whole series of notes that all have that same rhythmic value.
- Press caps lock and the QWERTY keys with Use MIDI Device for Input turned off to enter pitches without a MIDI keyboard.

Enharmonics
- Press 9 to change the note to its enharmonic spelling.
- Press ctrl-9 to change all notes in the measure to their enharmonic spellings.
- When working with chords, pressing 9 will cycle through other spellings of the chord. Keeping pressing 9 until you get the one you are looking for.

Arrow keys
- Press CTRL left arrow to move the insertion point to the first note or rest in the Speedy editing frame.
- Press CTRL right arrow to move the insertion point just beyond the last entry in the Speedy editing frame.

Exercise 1.2
How would you create the following using the Speedy Entry Tool?
- Hidden notes
- Enharmonic Notes
- Broken Stems
- Flipped Stems
- Ties
- Grace notes
- Flipped Ties
- Flat Beams/Slanted Beams

Do the same music now using the Speedy Entry Tool **without** MIDI.
Exercise 1.3

Putting It All Together:

- Open the "Grand Staff" template from the template folder.
- Ignore the slurs, trills, articulations and dynamics.
- Try to do as much as you can otherwise.
- Think about how you might do the tremolo in the left hand?

Tools covered in this chapter are listed below:

Selection Tool

Staff Tool

Speedy Entry Tool

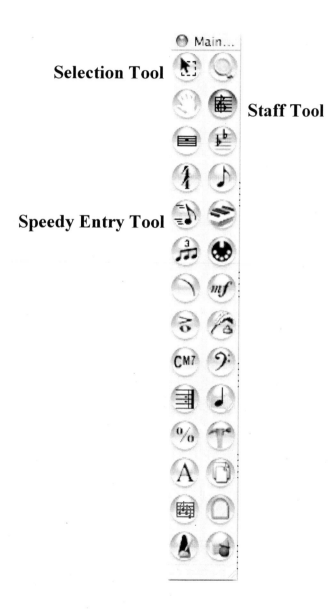

Speedy Entry Tool WITH MIDI

To enter music in step time using MIDI:

- Make sure your MIDI equipment is set up and configured properly-- check the MIDI menu to make sure.

- **Click the Speedy Entry Tool.** Check to make sure "Use MIDI Keyboard for Input" is selected under the Speedy Menu.

- **Click the first measure into which you want to enter music.** The Speedy Entry editing frame appears.

- **To enter a note or chord, hold down the desired key (or keys) on the synthesizer and press a number key on the computer keypad corresponding to the desired rhythmic value.**

- If you press a number key without holding down any synthesizer keys, a rest of the specified duration appears.

- If you want to insert a note, chord, or rest before the insertion bar, press shift as you press the number key.

- Press the period key to dot the note (you can add up to ten dots by repeating this action).

- If the next few notes you want to enter are part of a tuplet (a triplet, quintuplet, etc.), press option-number, where 3 means triplet, 5 means quintuplet, and so on.

- **To change the rhythmic value of a note or rest, position the insertion bar on it and press the number key corresponding to the desired value.** The following diagram again shows which keys correspond to which note values.

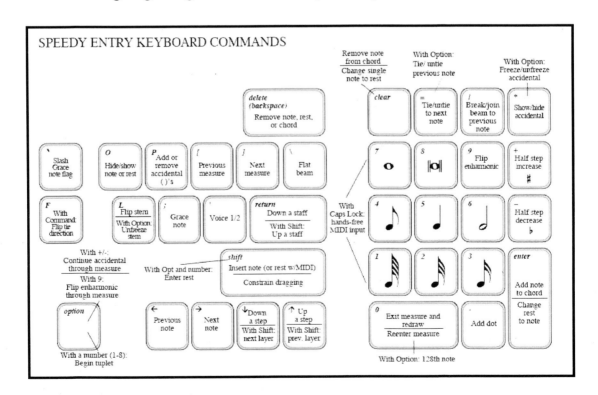

Try a little bit of the same music now using the Speedy Entry Tool **WITH** MIDI.

Exercise 2.1

Other Useful Speedy Options:

- **Speedy Frame: Scale to Staff**
  - **Minimum Percentage/Maximum Percentage:** Select this radio button to adjust the size of the Speedy Frame based on a combination of the view percentage and the size of the staff.
- **Speedy Frame: Use Fixed Scaling of:** Select the radio button to set the size of the Speedy Frame to a specific percentage.

- **Fill With Rests when Leaving Measure.**

- **Auto Launch Frame-** Speedy Entry Tool will open a measure for editing.

- **Use MIDI Keyboard for Input-** Same as under the Speedy Menu.

- **Use MIDI Modifier Keys when in MIDI Input Mode-** When Use MIDI Modifier key is checked, Finale will respond to MIDI signals to set the duration, tie notes, and other functions, as specified in the selected Key Map.

- **MIDI Modifier Assignments: [Key Map list] · Create Key Map · Edit Key Map · Delete Key Map.** Select a map of MIDI keys from the popup list to use, edit, or delete. (see below)

Edit MIDI Modifiers dialog box

The MIDI Modifiers dialog box allows you to use MIDI keys (such as keys on your MIDI keyboard or a sustain pedal) to set the duration of a note, navigate the score and other commands.

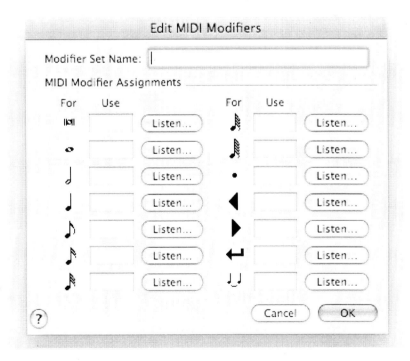

- **Modifier Set Name.** Enter a name for this definition of MIDI notes to use.

You can either type in a MIDI code or click "Listen…" and then play the MIDI event that you would like to assign to the following:

- **Note Duration**s
- **Dot**
- **Triangle Left (**moves the cursor backward one note or rest.)
- **Triangle Right (**moves the cursor forward one note or rest.)
- **Tied Notes**
- **Enter (**adds a note to a chord or turns a note into a rest).

Adding More Measures

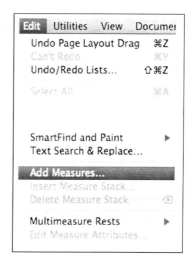

- Now found under the Edit menu.
- Select "Add Measures…"
- Select how many measures you want to add.

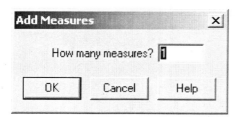

- **Insert Measure Stack:** Inserts *x* measures in all instruments **before** the measure you selected.
- **Delete Measure Stack:** Deletes the measure(s) you selected in all instruments.

 # Voice 1 & 2 in the Speedy Entry Tool

- **Click the Speedy Entry Tool and click a measure in which you want to enter music.**
- **Enter the notes of the first voice (Voice 1).**
- **Press the arrow keys to move the insertion point to the Voice 1 note at which the first Voice 2 note is to appear. (**Voice 2 musical line may materialize at any point in the measure, as long as it's been "launched" from an existing Voice 1 note. You can have several "launches" within a measure.
- **To enter Voice 2, press the apostrophe (') key.**
- **Enter the notes of the second voice (Voice 2).**

Example:

Use the "L" key to flip the stems if necessary. This can happen many ways, but is easy to correct. Use the ' key if the problem is in Voice 2 before you hit "L" key or you will change Voice 1 instead.

- Occasionally you may need to drag the notes left or right (for unisons or 2nds) so that you can see them properly.
- Rests work the same way in Voice 1 & 2.
- Often you must drag the rest out of the way of another note head or staff.

Example

Editing Voice 1 & 2

- Always remember that Voice 2 is linked to Voice 1 <u>**where you launched it.**</u>
- To make changes to Voice 2, you must switch to it using the ' key. Otherwise you will edit Voice 1.
- You can also change to Voice 2 by clicking on a Voice 2 note with the mouse.

 # Layers and the Speedy Entry Tool

The difference between Layers and Voice 1 & 2:
- <u>Layers are independent.</u> You can have any combination such as only layer 4 or layer 2 and 3.
- They are <u>not</u> linked to specific notes.
- Cannot edit a layer if it isn't currently selected (bottom left of screen 1234).
- Each layer can also have a voice 1 and 2.

To change layers:
- Click on the 1 2 3 4 on the bottom left corner of the screen

Or

- To cycle through the layers in Speedy Entry, click SHIFT ' (")(PC) or Shift Up-Arrow or Down-Arrow (Mac).

Example:

Layer Options:

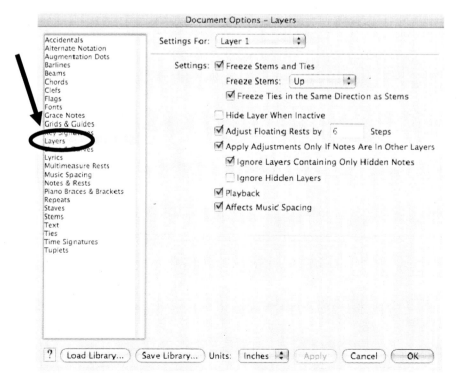

For each layer you can:
- Freeze Stems and Ties Up or Down.
- Adjust rests by so many steps so that they move out of the way automatically (use positive and negative values).
- Only apply adjustments if there are other layers with notes.
- Hide Layers when Inactive.
- Playback/Mute Layer.
- Turn off music spacing for a specific layer so it won't affect other layers.

Using Colors to Show Different Layers:

- Easy to see which layer is which for editing.
- Easy to see to which layer dynamics, articulations, etc. belong.

Moving Layers:
- Click the Selection Tool (Dashed Square with Arrow).
- Click on the Measure(s) you want to edit.
- Click Edit → Move/Copy Layers...
- Select which layer to move where. Be careful not to overwrite existing layers.
- Newer versions of Finale also let you copy one layer to another.

If you enter music in the wrong layer and notes are stemmed in the wrong direction, you can use "Move Layers" to easily correct the mistakes instead of flipping the stem of every note. In the example below, layer 1 was entered as layer 2 and layer 2 was entered as layer 1.

Example of using Move Layers:

Before: After moving layer 1 to layer 2 and
           layer 2 to layer 1:

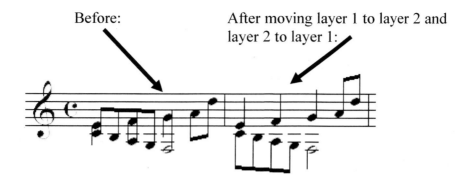

Showing & Editing Single Layers:

When this item is selected (displaying a check mark), Finale hides the three inactive layers. Hidden layers are unaffected by almost every tool. Music in a hidden layer won't be copied, pasted, or otherwise affected by edit operations—a useful fact to remember if you want to copy or paste the music of one layer only. Choose this command a second time to make the check mark disappear (and make the other three layers reappear).

Examples:

All Layers showing:

Showing Layer 1 only:

Showing Layer 2 only:

The Staff Tool- Adding More Staves

Uses:

To ADD a staff:
- Click the Staff Tool
- Double click in the music where you want to add the staff.

To DELETE a Staff:
- Click the Staff Tool
- Click the small square next to the staff you want to delete.
- Hit "BACKSPACE" or "DELETE" Key

To DELETE more than one staff:
- Click the Staff Tool
- Drag a box around the small squares of the staves you want to delete.

OR

- Hold down the SHIFT Key and Click the small squares next to all of the staves you want to delete.
- THEN
- Hit the "BACKSPACE" or "DELETE" Key to delete.

To ADD more than one staff:
- Click the Staff Tool
- Under the Staff Menu, Click New Staves...
- Enter the number of staves you want to add.
- Adjust the distance between staves if necessary.

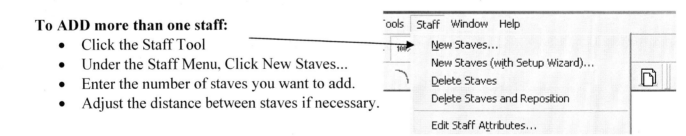

Other Options:

- **Delete Staves and Reposition**: Deletes the selected staves and moves the remaining ones up to fill in the space.

- **Respace Staves:** Changes the distance between all of the staves.

- **Sort Staves**: Fixes problems when you move staves above or below where they originally were.

- **Auto Sort Staves:** Automatically does a "Sort Staves" when you move a staff.

- **Staff Usage:** Browses and lets you edit each stave's position.

Staff | Window | Help

New Staves...
New Staves (with Setup Wizard)...
Delete Staves
Delete Staves and Reposition

Edit Staff Attributes...
Respace Staves...
Sort Staves
✔ Auto Sort Staves
Staff Usage...

Define Staff Styles...
Clear Staff Styles
Apply Staff Styles...
✔ Show Staff Styles

Putting It All Together:

Try the following example using voices and/or layers:

Chapter 3
More Notational Tools

Tools covered in this chapter are listed below:

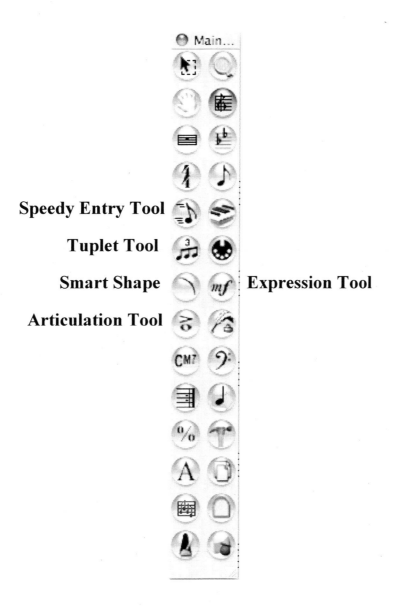

Speedy Entry Tool

Tuplet Tool

Smart Shape   Expression Tool

Articulation Tool

Creating Tuplets with the Speedy Entry Tool

Finale Terminology:

TUPLET: Any note or group or notes that is/are part of an irregular division of the beat such as triplets, quintuplets, sextuplets, etc. Tuplets of up to eight notes can be easily entered using the Speedy Entry Tool (see below). Tuplets of more than eight notes must be entered using the Tuplet tool. The Tuplet tool also allows you to fine-tune the appearance of your tuplets.

It's easy to creative Tuplets while in Speedy Entry mode:

- While in Speedy Entry Mode, press [OPTION] on Mac's or [CTRL] on PC's.
- Then press the number of tuplet you want to create. (For example, 3 for a triplet).
- Enter the notes that make up your tuplet.
- The first note duration you enter after you press option and the number, defines the tuplet. For example, if you press option 3 and then enter an eighth note, you will make an eighth note triplet.
- You can only create tuplets of up to eight notes in this manner. See using the tuplet tool (below) for creating larger tuplets.
- You can use the tuplet tool to customize and edit the tuplets you create this way.

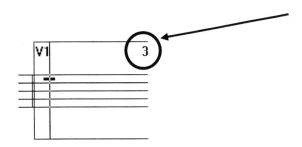

The number in the top right corner of the box shows you the tuplet number.

Example 3.1:

The Tuplet Tool

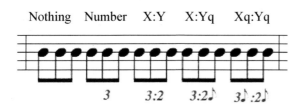

- Allows you to edit and define tuplets.
- Can create a tuplet by clicking on the note on which you want the tuplet to start.
- Define the tuplet using the number/duration of notes in the space of number/duration of notes. For example, 3 quarter notes in the space of 2 quarter notes.
- Make the appropriate changes in the Tuplet Definition Box for the appearance of the tuplet.

Placement Options:

Enhanced:	Number, Nothing, Ratio
Avoid Staff:	Always places brackets above the top line, or below the bottom line of the staff.
Allow Horizontal Drag:	Allows movement left/right not just up/down.
Use Bottom Note:	Positions tuplet values from bottom note of a chord.
Break Slur/Bracket:	Makes an opening for the number in the bracket.

Appearance Options:

Number:	Nothing, Number, Ratio as X:Y, X:Yq, or Xq:Yq (where "q" is the actual duration (quarter, eighth, etc. See below.)

Nothing   Number   X:Y   X:Yq   Xq:Yq

3   3:2   3:2♪   3♪:2♪

Shape:	Nothing, Bracket, Slur
Placement:	Manual, Stem/Beam Side, Note Side, Above, Below
Auto Bracket:	Draws a bracket/slur only if needed
Break Slur/Bracket:	Makes an opening for the number.

Other Options:
- Always Use Specified Shape.
- Never Bracket Beamed Notes on Beam Side.
- Bracket Unbeamed Notes Only.

To Edit or Delete a Tuplet, click on the note on which the tuplet starts and then either drag one of the handles (shown below), double click any of the handles to display the tuplet definition, or click one of the handles and then click delete to delete to tuplet.

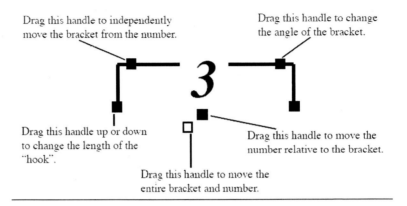

Example 3.2 using common tuplet options:

 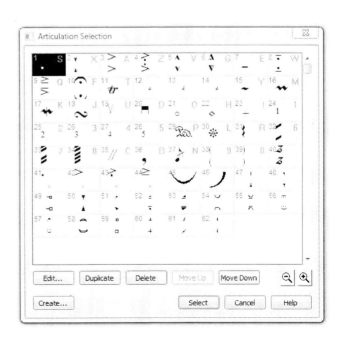

Articulation Tool

Point & Click Method:
1. Click the note on which you want to place an Articulation.
2. Choose the symbol from the window that pops up.
3. Adjust if necessary.

Drag Method

1. Drag a rectangle around the note(s) on which you want to place the same articulation.
2. Click "Select…" to choose the Articulation to place on the selected notes.
3. You can also specify to either apply the articulation to all notes or to just a specific range of durations including notes that end and/or start with a tie.

Metatools (Macros):

    Defining Metatools:
-   Click the Articulation tool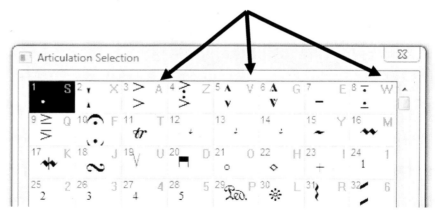
-   Hold down [SHIFT] and type the key you wish to assign the Metatool.
-   Click on the Articulation you want to use for that key.

    Using the Metatool:
-   Click the Articulation tool
-   Hold down the key to which you assigned the Metatool.
-   Click the note on which you want to place the Articulation.

You can tell what keys are assigned to which symbols by the number/letter in top right corner.

Articulation Example 3.3:

Creating a new symbol:
If you desire a symbol in another font that is not already in Finale, click "Create" in the Articulation Selection screen. Then you can select the font and main and flipped symbol to use in Finale. After you create a new symbol, it acts just like any other articulation.

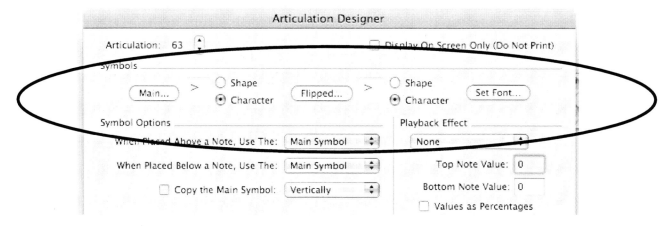

Adding Articulations in Simple Entry

- **Select a note and press numpad "*" or Option-"A" and press an articulation Metatool key** to add an articulation to the note. For example, A for an accent, S for staccato, etc. Click Select (or press Enter) to open the Articulation Selection dialog box where you can choose from a list of articulations. (Note the Metatool assignment appears in the upper right corner of each articulation in the Articulation Selection dialog box.)

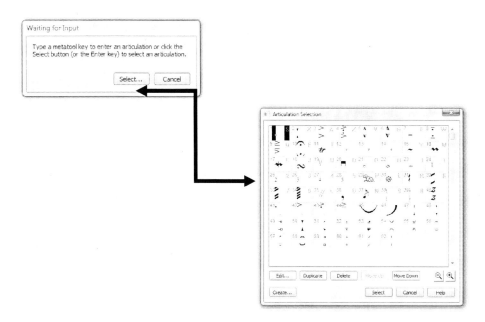

- **Press Command-numpad "*" or Command-Option-Shift-A and then press an articulation Metatool key** (or click select or press Enter to choose an articulation) to add a **sticky articulation** to the caret and mouse cursor. Now, the chosen articulation will appear on all notes entered until the sticky articulation is removed. Press Command-numpad * or Command-Option-Shift-A again to remove the articulation from the caret and mouse cursor.

Sticky Articulation

Special Mouse Clicks

- Click on, above, or below a note or rest to display the Articulation Selection dialog box, from which you can select an articulation marking you want to insert. (If you are using voices, click above the staff for Voice 1 and below for Voice 2.)

- Click or shift-click articulation handles to select one (or additional) articulations, respectively.

- Click and drag to select multiple handles.

- Press command-A to select all the handles.

- Drag a selected handle to move all selected articulations.

- Press delete, or control-click the handle and select Delete from the contextual menu to remove an articulation (or all selected articulations).

- Double-click an articulation handle (or select the handle and press return), or right-control-click the handle and select Edit Articulation Definition from the contextual menu to display the Articulation Designer dialog box, where you can edit the character used for an articulation marking, including its playback definition, font, and automatic-placement options.

- Drag-enclose a series of notes to bring up the Apply Articulation dialog box. Hold down delete and drag-enclose note to remove the articulations.

- Option-click and hold a handle of an articulation to highlight the note to which it is assigned.

Smart Shape Tool

Finale Terminology:

SMART SHAPE: Stretchable markings that shrink or expand as you widen or narrow the measure. You <u>DO NOT</u> need to have the specific shape (slur, crescendo, etc.) selected to edit it. You <u>DO NOT</u> need to have the specific layer active to edit it.

Slurs:
- Double Click on the first note of the slur.
- Move to the last note of the slur to highlight it.
- Use the Smart Shape menu if you need to change the slur's direction or press Apple-F to flip it.
- Use [OPTION] or [CTRL] to change the shape.

Crescendo/Decrescendo (hairpins):
- Double Click where you want the shape to start and drag to where it ends.

Trills:
- Double Click on the note where you want the trill to start.
- Drag the mouse to extend the wavy line.
- Use just the wavy line if you don't need the trill sign or for trill extension.

8va/15ma:
- Double Click on the note where you want to 8va/15ma to start and drag the mouse to extend the dotted line.
- If you place the 8va under notes, it will change to 8vb and 15ma will change to 15^{mv}.

Lines/Dotted Lines:
- Double Click on the note where you want the line to start.
- Drag the mouse to extend it.
- Can be used for Pedal Markings, 8va, etc.

Example 3.5:

Glissandi and Bends and Slides:

Glissandi - Guitar Bends - Hat Bends -TAB Slides - Smart Lines

Example 3.6:

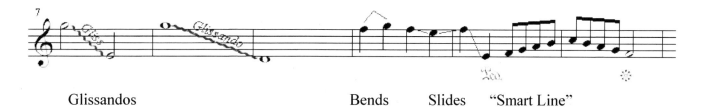

Glissandos   Bends   Slides   "Smart Line"

Using the Smart Line

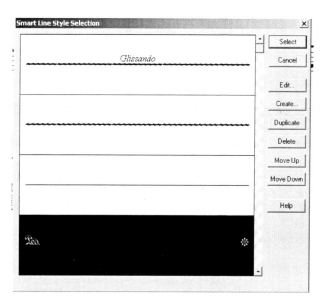

The "Smart Line" ? allows you to make a customizable line style or pick from one of the already defined styles. Hold down [OPTION] on Mac or [CTRL] on PC and click the "Smart Line" tool to change or create a line.

Some uses for the Smart Line are piano pedal markings, custom trills, custom lines and arrows, and text followed by dashed lines such as "rit. - - - - - - - - - - - -".

Example 3.7:
Other uses for the Smart Line:

Special Mouse Clicks

- Click the primary square handle of a Smart Shape in the score to select it and display the editing handles where you can move, stretch, or reshape the selected Smart Shape.
- Press the Tab key to select the next secondary handle when a shape is being modified.
- Press Ctrl-A to select all Smart Shapes on the page. Drag-select Smart Shape handles to select multiple Smart Shapes. Shift-click to add a Smart Shape to the selection.
- Click and drag (or use the arrow keys to nudge) a diamond editing handle on the tip of the slur to move the slur's endpoint and attach the slur to a different note.
- Click and drag (or use the arrow keys to nudge) a center curve diamond editing handle to change the slur's arc height. Shift-click and drag the arc handle to change the arc height and the angle of the arc.
- Drag or nudge an outer curve diamond editing handle to make asymmetrical changes to the slur's arc and inset. These two handles control the Bezier curve control points.
- Hold down Alt and drag an outer curve diamond editing handle for symmetrical changes to the slur's arc and inset.
- Hold down Shift while creating or editing a Smart Shape to constrain dragging.
- Press Alt and then double-click and drag a bracket Smart Shape to create an inverted bracket with the hook pointing away from the staff instead of toward the staff. It will also change the text for ottava's below or above the staff.
- Double-click or Ctrl-click the Custom Line Tool to bring up the Smart Line Selection dialog box.

 # Expression Tool

The Expression Tool is similar to the Articulation tool except that it allows you to attach more than one letter or symbol to either a note to a measure. These are called expressions. In versions up to and including 2003, an expression must be in only font-- you cannot mix music characters and regular text, for example.

Much has changed with the Expression Tool as you can see from the window below. No longer are there note and measure expressions. In Finale 2009, "note expressions" and "measure expressions" have been merged, and any expression can have properties of either. The major distinction between expression types is now based on their score function. Specifically, expressions have been separated into six categories, each with its own font, positioning, and Score List settings. Changes to these settings can be applied to all expressions in that category (both in the library and in the score). Score List definitions are now defined for categories rather than individual expressions, and are only available in categories that benefit from their usage.

To understand the benefits of this new model, it is important to recognize that all expressions are classified in one of two ways:

- Expressions that apply to the entire score (all staves): These include tempo markings, tempo alterations, and rehearsal letters. These expressions will generally appear on all parts, but only once, or a few times, in the score.

- Expressions that apply to a single staff: These include dynamics, expressive text, style markings, and technique text. Although more than one staff/part may require the same expression at the same measure, each of these types of expressions applies to their respective staff only.

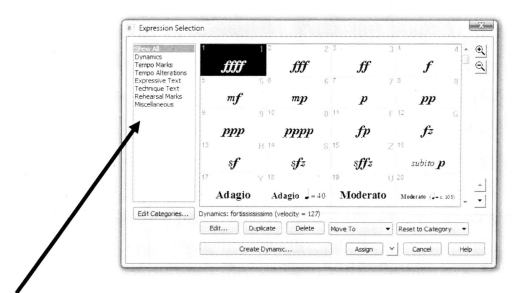

As shown in the column on the left of the Expression Selection window, Expressions are now broken up into categories and can have different characteristics based on what category they are in. Each category includes its own font, size, and style. When you create a new expression, Finale automatically assigns the category's font, size, and style to the text you type. Also, because some markings, particularly tempo marks, require multiple fonts, a category can include up to three different fonts, Text (e.g. Times New Roman), Music (e.g. Maestro), and Number.

Each category's positioning settings also apply to all expressions in the category. To accommodate markings that apply to the full score, but only appear on certain staves, some expression categories include a Score List. For example, tempo marks often appear above the top staff of a large score, as well as above the top staff in each instrumental section. Score Lists are also capable of automatically placing expressions properly in optimized scores, where various staves are hidden in some systems.

Changes to the Category Designer dialog box apply to all expressions in the selected category, including those that already exist in the score, except those specifically defined to ignore category settings.

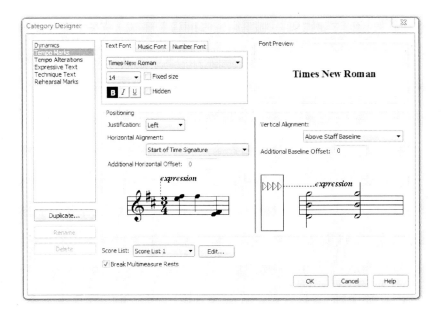

You can add expressions using the Point & Click Method or create Metatools as you can do with the Articulation tool. Most expressions will now position themselves properly in the music based on their type and usage.

 If you are using the Simple Entry Tool, you can quickly enter Expressions the same way as articulations: Select a note and press "X". This will then allow you to press an expression Metatool key to assign the expression.

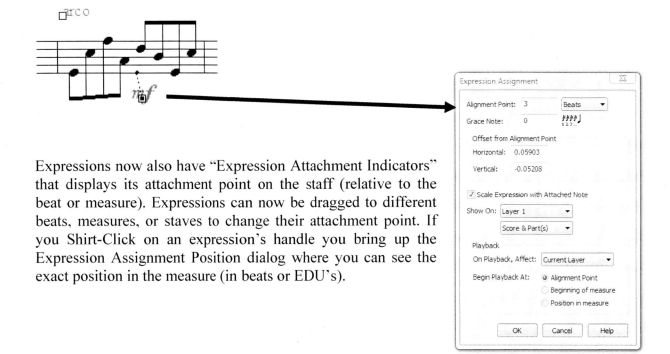

Expressions now also have "Expression Attachment Indicators" that displays its attachment point on the staff (relative to the beat or measure). Expressions can now be dragged to different beats, measures, or staves to change their attachment point. If you Shirt-Click on an expression's handle you bring up the Expression Assignment Position dialog where you can see the exact position in the measure (in beats or EDU's).

All Categories **except** for "Tempo Alterations" and "Rehearsal Marks" can be assigned to a single staff, multiple staves, or all staves by clicking the " 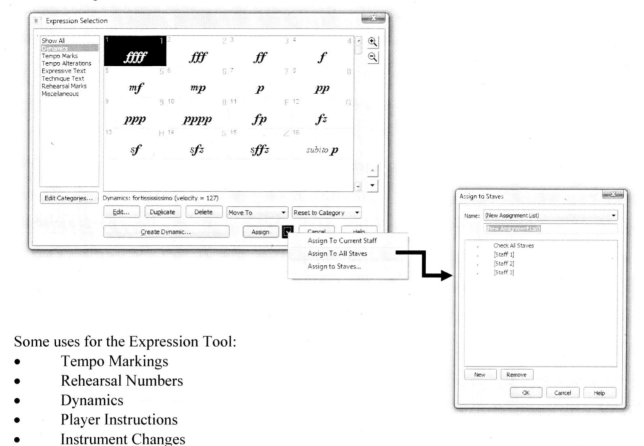 " symbol and choosing the needed option.

Some uses for the Expression Tool:
- Tempo Markings
- Rehearsal Numbers
- Dynamics
- Player Instructions
- Instrument Changes
- Technique Changes

Enclosing Expressions

You can also "Enclose" Expressions in a variety of shapes as show in Example 3.8 by clicking "Enclose Expression…"

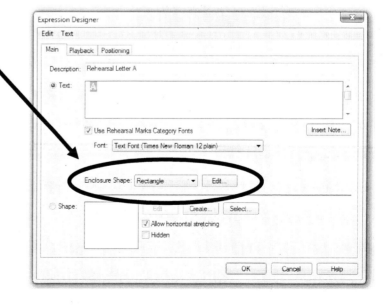

Then choose your shape and any other settings:

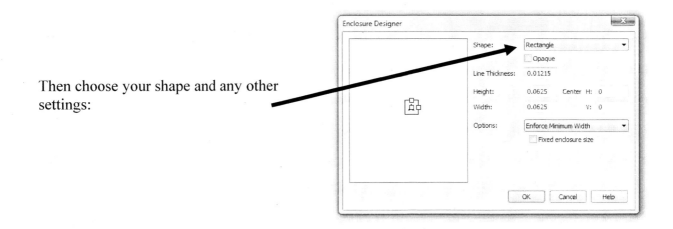

Example 3.8:

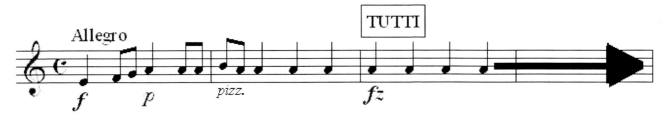

The Shape Designer: Creating Your Own Shapes

If Finale doesn't have the musical symbol you want, or you just want to create your own unique symbol, you can easily do it with the Shape Designer:

- Create a new Expression of any category.

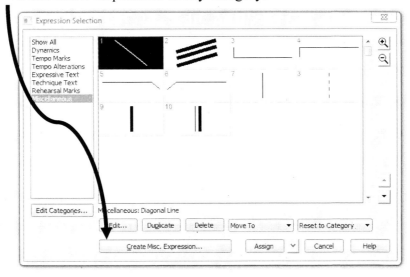

- Change the type from "Text" to "Shape"

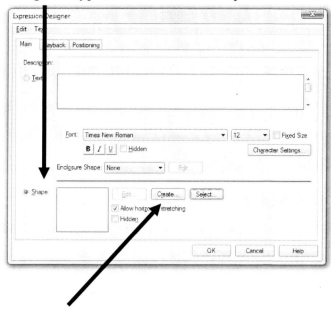

- Click "Create…" to create a new shape. This brings up the **Shape Designer.**

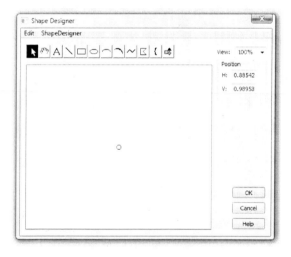

The **Shape Designer** is a basic drawing program. You can draw text, lines, squares/rectangles, circles/ovals, arcs, slurs, polygons, brackets/braces, and even import graphics.

Click on the tool you would like to use and start drawing.

There are other options under the Shape Designer menu to specify line style, line thickness, arrowheads, shape fill. You can also change the order of shapes and group and ungroup objects here.

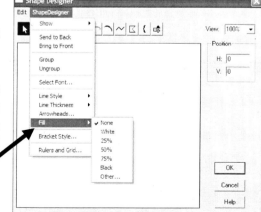

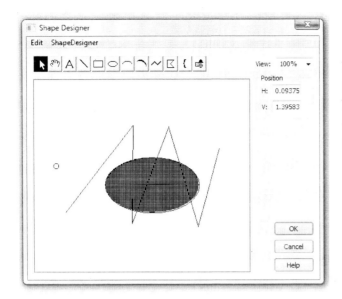

Use the drawing tools to make the symbol you want to create in Finale. This tool is very useful for aleatoric and contemporary music where arrows and unique shapes are often employed.

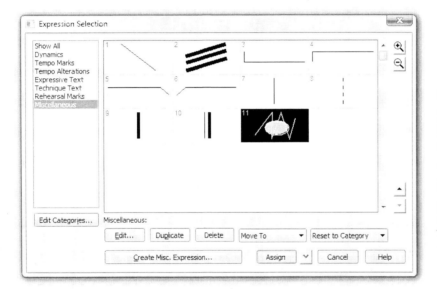

Once you have finished your drawing in the Shape Designer, click "OK" and your drawing will be turned into an Expression that can be placed into your music just like any other Expression.

Articulation Example 3.4:

You can make your own shapes   or use text or symbols.

Putting it all together:

Using what you have learned so far, reproduce the following score:

Some things to think about:
- Use the Staff Tool to add more staves.
- Set the time signature to 6/8. (Hide the time signature in the first measure if you want your music to look exactly like the score below).
- For now, use the Clef Tool to change the starting clef for the viola and cello.
- Use the Articulation Tool to add the staccato dots.
- Use the Smart Shape Tool to add the slurs, crescendos, and decrescendos.
- Use the Expression Tool to add the dynamics.

Tools covered in this chapter are listed below:

Selection Tool

Measure Tool

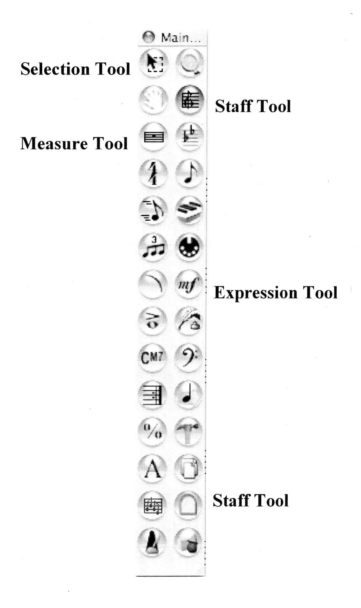

Staff Tool

Expression Tool

Staff Tool

Document Setup Wizard

The Document Setup Wizard makes it easy to set up simple and complex scores by just answering four screens:

Step 1:

- Select a preconfigured ensemble or create your own custom ensemble of instruments.
- Select a document style (font, cover page, and expression placement, staff spacing, etc.)
- Select Score and Part page size.

Step 2:

- If you chose an existing ensemble in Step 1, your instruments will already be chosen. Otherwise, select the Instrument Set (for playback) and the sound you want for each staff.
- Choose Score Order.
- Select if you want to link your parts to the score.

Step 3:

- Enter Title, Subtitle, Composer, Arranger, Lyricist, and Copyright information.
- All of these fields are optional. So fill in only what you want to appear on the score.

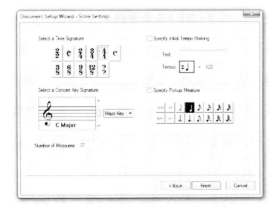

Step 4:

- Specify the Time Signature, Key Signature, Initial Tempo Marking, Pickup Measure, and number of measures.

Measure Tool

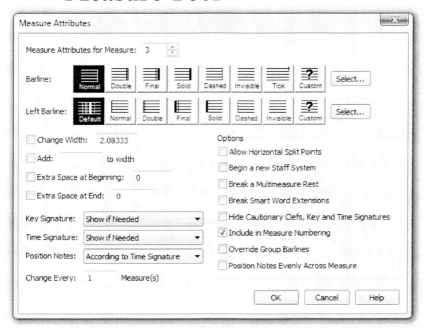

- Allows you to specify special right and left barlines such as double bar, final bar, no barline, etc.
- Allows you to Hide or Show the Key Signature and Time Signature.
- Allows you to specify the measure width.
- Allows you to Position Notes according to:
    - Time Signature
    - Manually
    - Beat Chart Spacing

Other Options:

- Hide Cautionary Clefs, Key, and Time Signatures.
- Position Notes evenly Across Measure (for when there are too many or too few notes according to the time signature).
- Begin a new Staff System (moves the measure to the next line).
- Break a multi-measure Rest.
- Allow Horizontal Split Points (for breaking a really long measure in the middle for a new line).
- Override Group Barlines.

If you select more than one measure, you can use the "**Change Every** _____ **Measure(s)**" to change measures based on a pattern.

If your music contains measures with greater or fewer beats than the time signature specifies (in a solo or cadenza, for example), you may need to click "Position Notes Evenly Across Measure" as shown in Example 4.1 for the music to be spaced properly.

Example 4.1:

Without "Position Notes Evenly Across Measure"

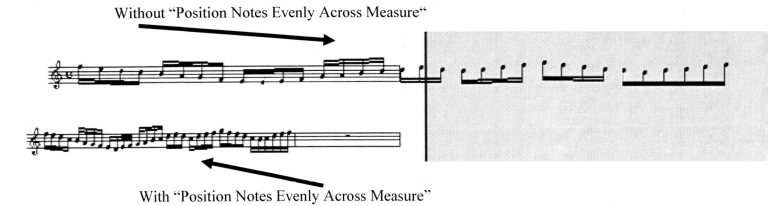

With "Position Notes Evenly Across Measure"

Exercise 4.2
Try this example of using different barlines:

 **Special Mouse Clicks**

- Double-click the Measure Tool to add a single new blank measure at the end of the score.
- Ctrl-click the Measure Tool to display the Add Measures dialog box.
- Ctrl-click the measure handle to display all measure numbers defined for a measure (even if no numbers are currently showing in the measure).

Making Groups and Brackets

If you did not use the Document Setup Wizard or want to group your staves manually, you will need to use the Staff Tool.

With the Staff Tool selected, Click Staff menu → Add Group and Bracket.

This will bring up the Group Attributes screen:

Options:

- Pick the staff you want to start the group and the staff in which you want the group to end. **OR,** Select the staves you want to group <u>before</u> you select "Add Group and Bracket…"
- Choose if the barline goes on staves, through staves, or between staves.
- Choose any optional barline style.
- Choose the bracket to show the group.
- Define Group Name, Abbreviated Group Name and Position(s) (optional).

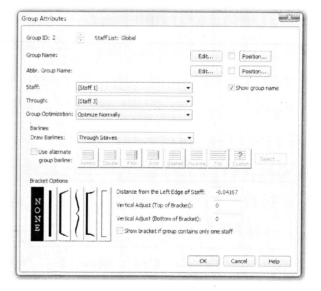

Example 4.3.a (for Piano):

Example 4.3.b (for 4 voice choir):

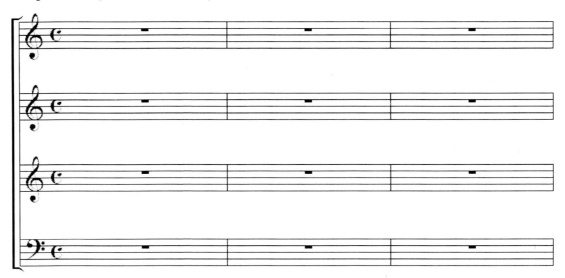

Example 4.3.c (for String Quartet):

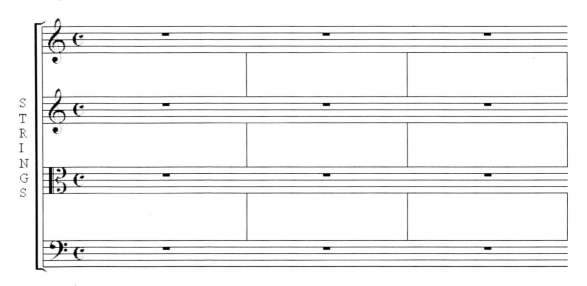

Staff Attributes:

The Staff Attributes screen allows you to customize a staff. If you used the Document Setup Wizard, most of this is taken care of for you.

To edit the attributes for any staff, double click anywhere on the staff that you want to edit.

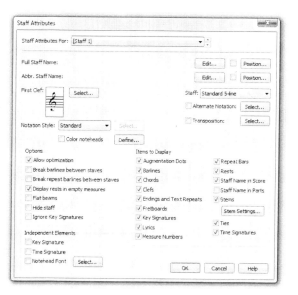

Options:

- Enter Full Name and Abbreviated Name and their positions on the screen.

- Enter starting clef.

- Enter any automatic transposition.

- Change from a 5 line staff to a one line or other line staff.

- Select which items to display. (You may want to hide some items from the second staff for piano music for instance.)

- **Independent Elements:** Make Key Signature, Time Signature, and Notehead Font different from other staves.

- Change the notation style (regular, percussion, note shapes, tablature).

- Allow Optimization (hide from score when empty). You may want to turn this **off** if you always want to make this staff show in your score. Finale will not hide it if it contains no music.

- Break Barlines/Repeat Barlines between staves (often used for choral music).

- Display Rests in Empty measures (Turn off and you have instant manuscript paper).

- Use Flat Beams.

- Hide entire staff.

- Ignore key signature (for timpani parts, for example).

Working with Transposing Instruments:

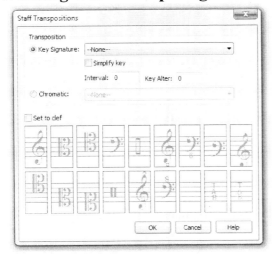

Options:

- **Transpose by Key Signature:** Used for tonal music when you have a key signature. Choose the key of the transposing instrument.
- **Specify a different interval and key change:**
    - **Interval** is the number of lines and spaces to raise or lower the note.
    - **Key Alter** is the number of sharps to add (positive number) or number of flats to add (negative number)
        - **Simplify Key** changes the key to one with less sharps or flats (In the key of B Major, transposing up a major 2nd would be the key D-flat would be used instead of the key of C-sharp)
- **Transpose Chromatic:** Used for non-tonal music. No change is made to the key signature. Accidentals are placed in the music as needed.
- You can also have the transposed music change clef. For example, to force a French Horn to always be in treble clef even if you wrote parts in bass clef.

Displaying the Score in Concert Pitch:

If you want to work in concert pitch or to toggle back and force between viewing your score in concert pitch and transposed, click "Display in Concert Pitch" under the Document menu.

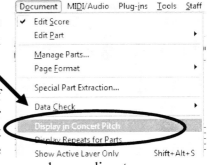

NOTE:

This option is also important when you are entering music. If "Display in Concert Pitch" is not turned on, notes you enter for transposing instruments, will be the written (transposed) note, not the sounding note. If you turn on "Display in Concert Pitch," the notes you enter will be the actual sounding notes before they are transposed according to the staff's transposition settings.

Exercise 4.4

Set up the following score with the correct transpositions.

Make sure you have "Display in Concert Pitch" selected first.

Then turn off "Display in Concert Pitch" to see the music transposed:

Using "Staff Sets" for Easier Viewing of Large Scores

Finale Terminology:

STAFF SET: A user defined custom view of your score. You can specify only which staff or staves you wish to view using a Staff Set. Any spacing changes you make to staves in a Staff Set <u>do not</u> affect the spacing of the actual score layout. Staff sets easily allow you to work with staves that are not close to each other in normal score order. You can define up to 8 staff styles per document.

To define a Staff Set:

- Choose the staves to be in the set by selecting them with the Staff Tool either by clicking their handles or dragging a selection around their handles .
- Hold down [OPTION] (MAC) or [CTRL] (PC) and go to View → Select Staff Set → Staff Set 1,2,3,etc.

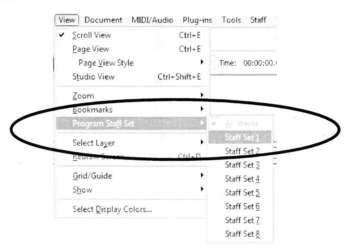

Exercise 4.5

- Make a score with 10 staves.
- Name the top one "Flute".
- Name the last one "Violin".
- With the Staff Tool, Click the handle box next to the Flute.
- Scroll down to the Violin staff.
- Hold down [SHIFT] and click the square next to it.
- Hold down [OPTION] or [CTRL] and go to the menu View → Program Staff Set → Staff Set 1

Notes:

- You can create up to 8 Staff Sets.
- You can change and redefine existing ones.

Music Spacing

Gone are the days that you had to manually apply spacing to measures using the now retired **Mass Mover Tool.** Music spacing is now elegantly handled by Finale automatically if you have "Automatic Music Spacing" turned on... which it is by default. If you wish to manually space your music, you can always turn off the automatic spacing by unchecking this option (see below). You can, however, apply different music spacing with the Select Tool so it is still worthwhile to know and understand how music spacing works.

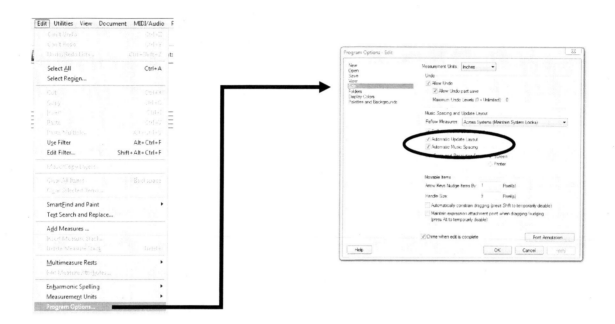

Music Spacing Options:

Apply Beat Spacing (Metatool "4") -- Finale calculates the position of each beat in the measure according to the ratio or table of widths; any notes within the beat are spaced linearly (where an eighth note gets exactly half as much space as a quarter note, and so on).

Apply Note Spacing (Metatool "5") -- Finale calculates the precise position of each note based on its ratio or the table of widths. This command provides more exact spacing than does the Beat Spacing command; both result in a striking, beautifully laid-out score. (Finale uses Note Spacing when Automatic Music Spacing is being used.)

You can also choose **Apply Time Signature Spacing,** which restores notes to linear spacing, where a half note gets exactly twice as much space as a quarter note. Time Signature Spacing is what Finale uses when you first put notes into the score when Automatic Music Spacing is not being used. Because Time Signature Spacing is linear, the Collision Avoidance options in Document Options-Music Spacing are ignored.

 ### Selection Meta Tools 4 & 5

Exercise 4.6
To Apply Beat Spacing (Meta Tool 4)
- Select the Selection Tool .
- Select all the measures you want to change.
- Press "4" or go under the Utilities menu and choose "Music Spacing"→ "Apply Beat Spacing".

With Beat spacing:

Exercise 4.7
To Apply Note Spacing (Meta Tool 5):
- Select the Selection Tool .
- Select all the measures you want to change.
- Press "5" or go under the Utilities menu and choose "Music Spacing"→ "Apply Note Spacing".

With Note Spacing:

Exercise 4.8
To Apply Time Signature Spacing:
- Select the Selection Tool .
- Select all the measures you want to change.
- Go under the Utilities menu and choose "Music Spacing"→ "Apply Time Signature Spacing".

With Time Signature Spacing:

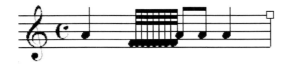

Note:
When you change the way the music is spaced, the handles in the Measure Tool  change how the notes are moved.

Examples of Spacing:

Example 4.9

Using Time Signature Spacing

> When the music is spaced using Time Signature Spacing, there is only one handle which controls the width of the measure.

Example 4.10

Using Beat Spacing (with Beat Chart)

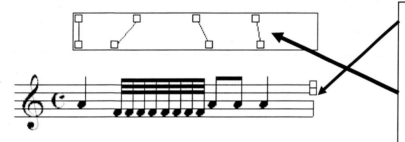

> Click here to show Beat Chart.
>
> Drag the lower squares of the beat chart to move the beats left or right. Double click between the upper squares to add another beat marker.

Example 4.11

Using Note Spacing (with Note Chart)

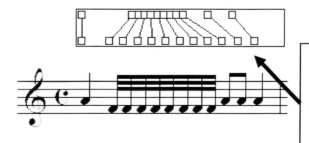

> When the music has Note Spacing, each note has a corresponding handle in the Note Chart.
>
> Moving the handle left or right will move that portion of the beat left or right **for all staves**.

Expression Tool- Making Score Lists

Depending on which category your Expression is, you will be able to define Score Lists which tell Finale in which staff or staves in the score and part to show the Expression. Tempo Marks, Tempo Alterations, and Rehearsal Marks all use Score Lists.

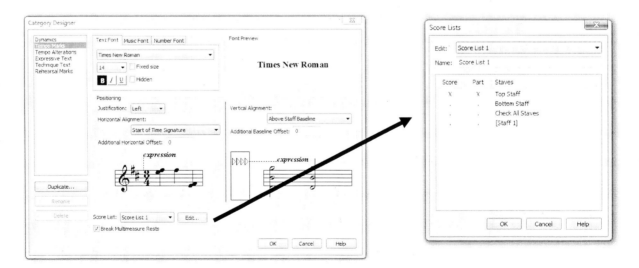

In the Category Designed screen, click "Edit" next to Score List.
Here you can create a new Score List or edit an existing Score List.
Create a name for your list and select whether this group of expressions will be shown on the score and/or parts on:
- **Top Staff**
- **Bottom Staff**
- **All Staves**
- **Specific Staves**

Individual Positioning:

Unlike other earlier versions of Finale, all Expressions except the Master Expression (see above) move independently of one another for easy positioning. The Master Expression moves all Expressions in all staves of the score and parts. If you need to move the Master Expression, hold down "`" (reverse apostrophe key below tilde) to do so.

If you wish to erase all of the position changes to the Expressions in a Score including the Master Expression, Right Click on the Expression's handle and click "Remove Manual Adjustments." This will reset the Expression's position in all staves to that of the Master Expression.

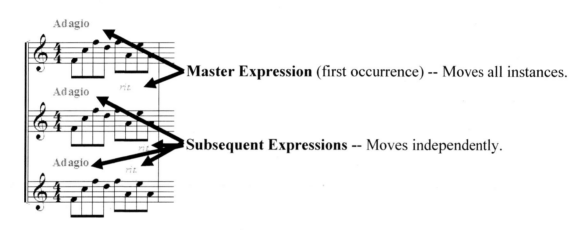

Master Expression (first occurrence) -- Moves all instances.

Subsequent Expressions -- Moves independently.

Putting it all together:

Using everything you know set up the score below.

Things to think about:
- Different Time Signatures (Independent Elements).
- Groups & Brackets.
- Different Barlines.
- Enclosed Expressions.
- Staff Lists.
- Expressions with different positioning.

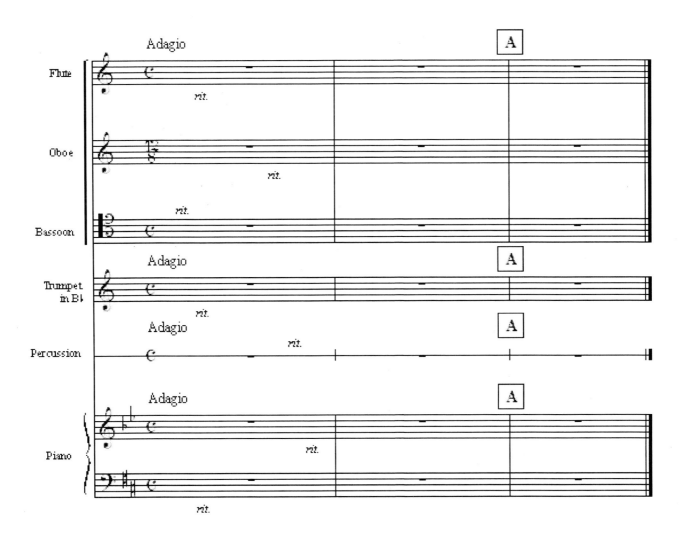

Chapter 5
Chords, Lyrics, and Repeats

Tools covered in this chapter are listed below:

Selection Tool

Measure Tool

Lyric Tool

Chord Tool

Repeat Tool

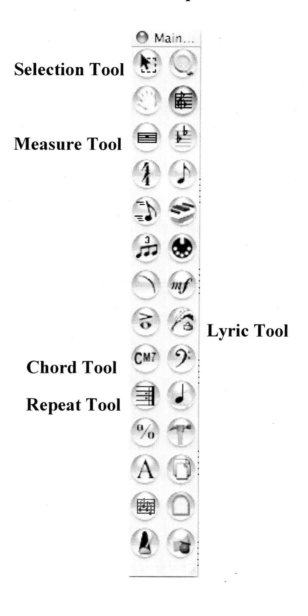

Measure Numbers

The Measure Tool is also used to easily put measure numbers anywhere in your piece. To number your measures, you need to create a region that contains all the measures you want to number. Using different regions allows you to restart or change the numbering in the middle of the piece or to start numbering with a number other than one.

- **Region-** Allows you to define several different numbering patterns in your piece. This can be useful if you have sections of music where the measure numbers stop.
- **Style-** Allows you to pick from several styles using numbers or letters.
- **Enclosures-** Like Expressions, you can enclose the measure number in a shape on every number or on selected numbers.
- **Positioning & Display-** Specifies where and how often the measure number appears.

To create a measure number region: With the Measure Tool selected, select the Measure Menu → Measure Numbers → Edit Regions. Then click "Add" to create a new region.

To Add a single measure number where there isn't one: With the Measure Tool selected, select the measure where you want to put a number, then select Measure Menu → Measure Numbers → Show Number.

To move or delete a measure number: Click the Measure Tool and drag the measure number to where you want it or click the measure number's handle and hit Delete.

Example 5.1:

Make this example of Measure Numbers:
To see the whole score as shown here: click View → Page View.

Here's how:
- Create a Measure Number Region from 1 to 10.
- Click Show Every 2 measures starting with measure 2.
- Set Enclosures to "Square" on every number.
- Click OK.
- With the measure tool selected, click measure 5 then click Measure Menu → Measure Numbers → Show Number.
- Create a second Measure Number Region from 11 to 999.
- Set the "First measure in region" to 100.
- Click to show at the beginning of each staff system.
- Click OK.

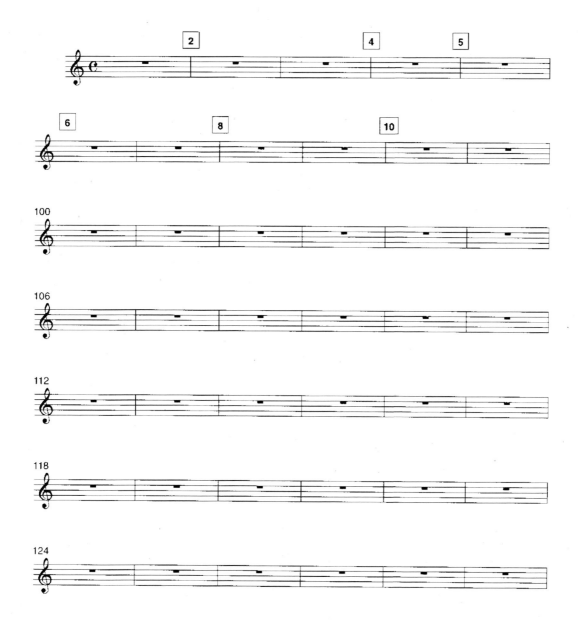

Repeat Tool

The Repeat Tool is used to put repeat bars and repeat endings in your piece. It also can control the playback of your piece to follow the "roadmap" created from the repeats (see chapter 10 for more on defining repeats for playback). For now, we are only concerned with creating repeats in the printed music.

You can place Graphic Repeat symbols as well as first and second endings.

You can also make text repeats that instruct the player to go to different places in the music.

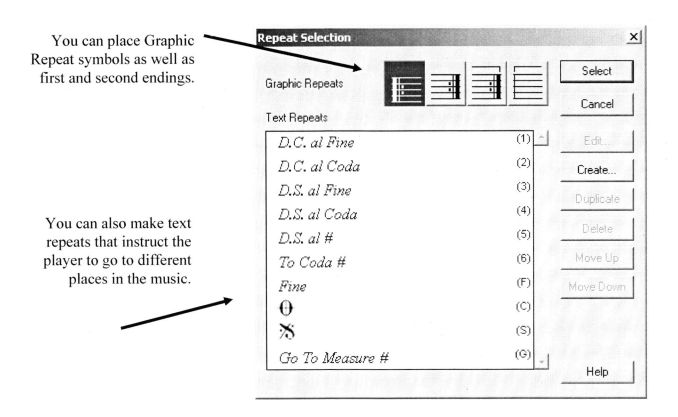

To place repeat bars in your piece: Click the Repeat Tool and then click the measure in which you want to place the repeat. Then choose what repeat graphic you want.

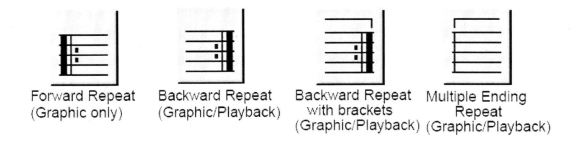

Example 5.2:

Simple Repeat: **Forward Repeat**   **Backward Repeat**

Example 5.3
Repeat with first and second ending:

Forward Repeat   **Multiple Ending Repeat**

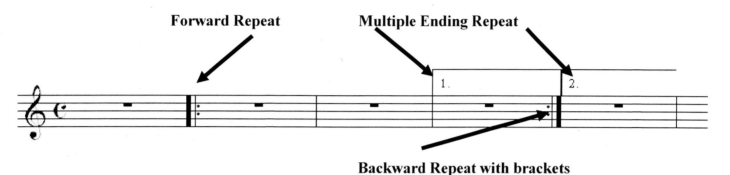

Backward Repeat with brackets

To create endings, place both the Multiple Ending Repeat **and** the Backward Repeat with brackets in the measures as shown below.

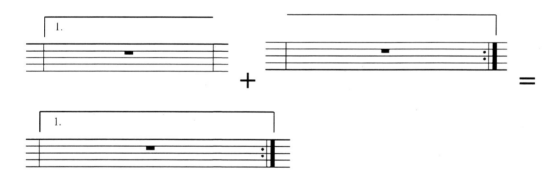

Newer versions of Finale can automatically create the backward repeat bar when you create the ending if "Create backward repeat bar" is checked.

If you highlight all of the measures that you want in your ending and then double-click on one, Finale will put the Backward Repeat Bar on the last selected measure. If there are many measures, you will, however, need to connect the repeat bracket manually as shown below. If you do not want Finale to create the Backward Repeat Bar when you make an ending, make sure to uncheck this option.

Finale for Composers

If your ending is more than one measure, you may have to extend the ending bracket to span all of the measures as shown below. To do so, click in the measure with the repeat and drag the corresponding handle to lengthen the bracket.

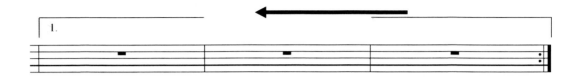

Multi-Measure First Ending:

Each part of the repeat bracket and also the ending number has a handle that you can use to fine tune the look of the repeat. You will often need to make the top line higher so that the music will fit under it.

In addition to Graphic Repeats, you can also use Text Repeats for such things as Codas, D.S. al Fine

Example 5.4
D.S. al Fine:

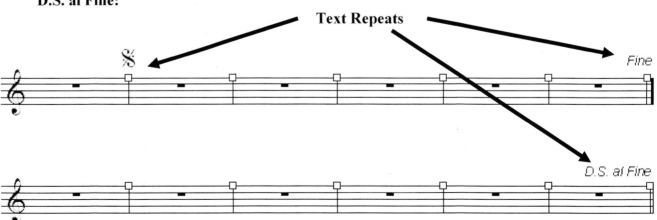

Example 5.5
D.S. al Coda:

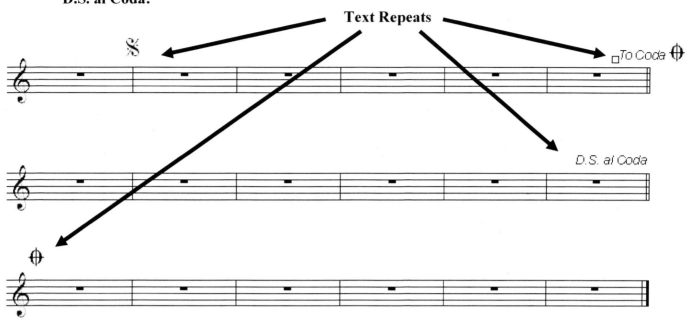

All of these repeats can also be used to affect the MIDI playback of your piece. But for now, just disregard the "Repeat Assignment" window that pops up after you choose your repeat.

 Special Mouse Clicks

- Double-click a measure to display the Repeat Selection box, where you can create either a repeat barline or a text repeat to insert into the score (and define it for playback, if you wish).
- Click a text repeat handle to select it; shift-click to select an additional one. Press Delete to remove any selected text repeats.
- Drag a text repeat handle to move the text repeat in any direction (in all staves simultaneously).
- Click a repeat barline handle to select it; press delete to remove it.
- Drag a repeat barline bracket handle up or down to make the bracket taller.
- Double-click a text repeat handle to display the Text Repeat Assignment dialog box, where you can change the spelling, font, or justification of the text repeat.
- Double-click a repeat barline handle (or its bracket handle) to display its Repeat Bar Assignment dialog box, where you can change the playback effects of the repeat barline.

Lyric Tool

The Lyric Tool is used to easily put lyrics into music. Each syllable or word is attached to a particular note and moves when that note moves.

There are two ways to get your lyrics into the score.

- **Type into Score**
- **Click Assignment**

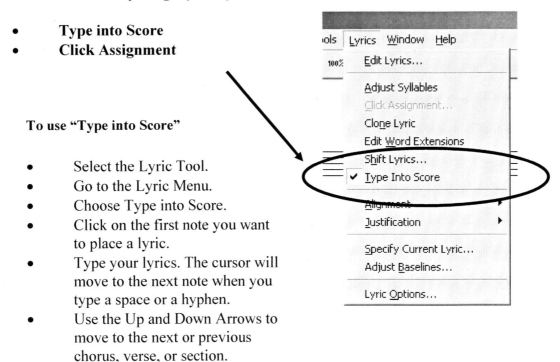

To use "Type into Score"

- Select the Lyric Tool.
- Go to the Lyric Menu.
- Choose Type into Score.
- Click on the first note you want to place a lyric.
- Type your lyrics. The cursor will move to the next note when you type a space or a hyphen.
- Use the Up and Down Arrows to move to the next or previous chorus, verse, or section.

Example 5.6:

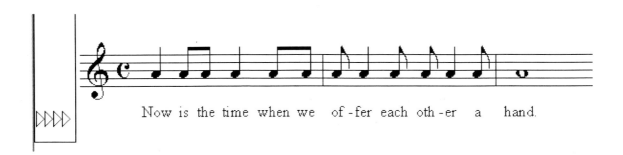

Click Assignment Method:

- Select the Lyric Tool.

- Go to the Lyric Menu.

- Choose "Edit Lyrics..."

- Type your lyrics free form (see right).

- Click "OK".

- Go to the Lyric Menu.

- Choose "Click Assignment"

- Click on the notes to assign your lyrics to them.

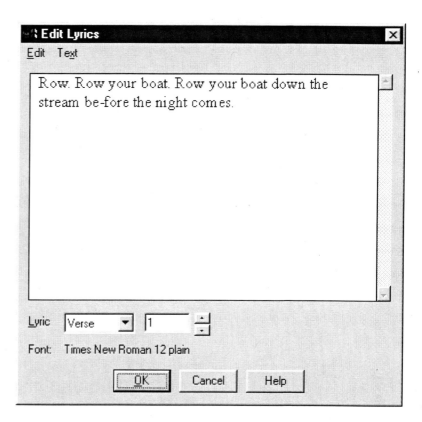

If you click **"Auto Update"** the music will automatically be spaced to accommodate the words.

If you hold down [OPTION] (Mac) or [CTRL] (PC) when you click your first lyric assignment, all of the lyrics will be automatically assigned according to the notes.

Exercise 5.7 using Click Assignment:

Word Extensions:

To create a Word Extension:
- Under the Lyric Menu, click Edit Word Extensions.
- Double Click on the NOTE above the word you want to add or edit the word extension. (In some versions of Finale, the box appears without having to click the note).
- Drag the handle right or left to increase or decrease the length of the word extension.

Exercise 5.8 using Word Extensions

Word Extension   Word Extensions

Adjusting individual words or syllables:
- Click the Lyric menu and choose "Adjust Syllables".
- Click on the NOTE that has the word you want to adjust.
- Move the word or syllable where you want it.

Example 5.9

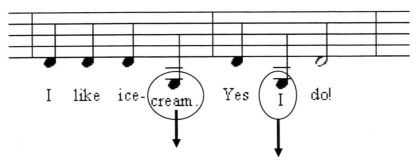

Move these down so that they don't run into the notes.

Clone lyrics:

You can clone lyrics so all occurrences of them will change if you edit the master lyric.

- Click the Lyric menu and choose "Clone Lyric".
- Click on the measure with the lyrics that you want to clone.
- Drag it to the measure where you want the lyrics copied.
- The lyrics will be copied note for note to the new measure.

Example 5.10

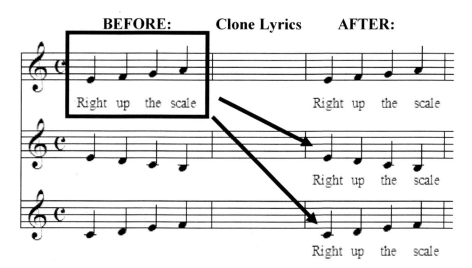

Be careful when Cloning Lyrics. Any changes you make to lyrics that you have cloned will affect the lyrics of all other instances at that same lyric. The only way to "unclone" lyrics is to use "Clear Items…" with the Selection Tool and specify lyrics to remove the lyrics.

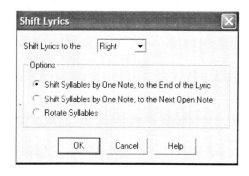

Shift Lyrics:

Use this dialog box to shift syllables right or left by one note.

Options:

Shift Syllables by One Note, to the End of the Lyric:
Shifts every syllable in the lyric set, beginning with the note you click either left or right.

Example 5.11
Original: **Shifted Right to End of Lyric:**

After clicking on the first note in the measure on the left, you can see that all the lyrics have moved to the right by one note.

Shift Syllables by One Note, to the Next Open Note:
Shifts syllables in the lyric set only as far as the next note that has no syllable attached.

Example 5.12
Original: **Shifted Right to Next Open Note:**

After clicking on the first note in the measure on the left, you can see that only the first four lyrics move one note to the right. All of the other lyrics remain where they were.

Rotate Syllables:
Replaces the syllable on each note with the syllable to its right or left—without changing which notes actually have lyrics.

Example 5.13
Original: **Rotated:**

After clicking on the first note in the measure on the left, you can see that the second note begins the lyric set again. Due to its unpredictable results and doubling of lyrics, this option is rarely used.

 **Special Mouse Clicks**

- Click a staff to tell Finale on which staff you want lyrics attached.
- In "Type Into Score," use the up and down arrows to move to the previous or next verse, chorus or section.
- Shift-click when working with lyrics in Voice 2.
- In "Type Into Score" or "Click Assignment," drag the positioning triangles at the left edge of the screen to specify the vertical position of the baseline for the lyric set you're inserting.
- In "Type Into Score mode," click near a note to select the syllable attached to it. Anything you now type replaces the highlighted syllable.
- In "Edit Word Extensions," press Delete to remove the word extension.
- In "Adjust Syllables," press backspace to restore a syllable to its original position or delete to remove it from the score.

 # Chord Tool

The Chord Tool allows you to place chord symbols and even guitar fret boards in your music.

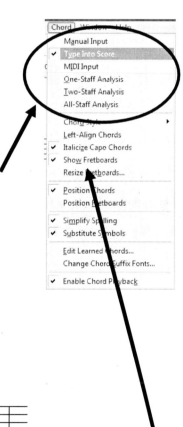

There are now six different ways to put chord symbols in your score.

You can show chord symbols, fret boards, or a combination of both:

Example 5.14
Chord symbols only:

To show fret boards, click "Show Guitar Fretboards" under the Chord Menu.

Example 5.15
Chord symbols and fret boards.

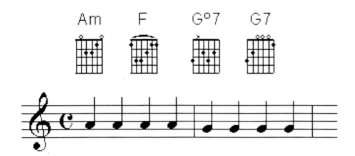

Method #1: Manual Input:

- With the Chord Tool selected, select "Manual Input" under the Chord Menu.
- Click on the note you want to place the chord.
- Then define the chord as shown below.

Enter the chord
Symbol here:

Define Fretboards
here:

This section defines
what is displayed.

This section sets
what is played.

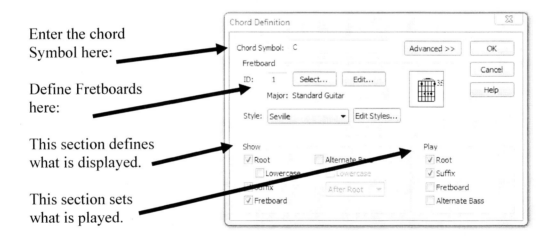

If you press "Advanced >>"
you can also enter
a chord by "Numeric
Definition."

Select a root, bass, and
suffix or by having Finale
listen while you those parts
of the chord.

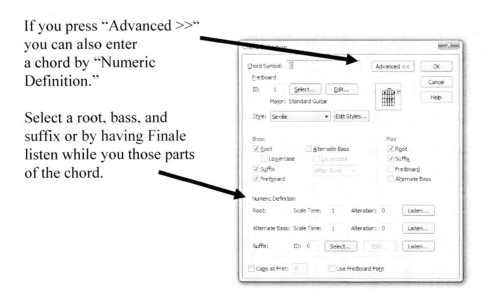

Exercise 5.16
Do this example using Manual Input:

Method #2: Type Into Score:

- This method functions much the same way as putting lyrics into your score with the Lyric Tool.
- Click the Chord Tool and select "Type into Score" from the Chord Menu.
- Click on the note where you want to add a chord.
- Type the chord symbols you want. Hit space to go to the next note.
- Finale then matches them against the chords that it already knows.
- If you enter a chord Finale doesn't understand, it will ask you if you want Finale to learn that chord spelling.

Exercise 5.17
Try the same example but use "Type Into Score"

When using "Type Into Score," Use these special symbols for Chords:

b	Displays flat symbol (lower case B).
#	Displays sharp symbol (shift 3).
o	Displays diminished symbol (lower case O).
%	Displays half-diminished symbol (shift 5).
/	Puts alternate bass note next to the chord root (slash).
_	Puts alternate bass note below the chord root (shift-hyphen).
,	Distinguishes the chord root from the suffix (comma).
:#	Displays the chord suffix assigned to a specific slot number in the Chord Suffix Selection dialog box (colon number).
|	Puts alternate bass note below and to the right of the chord root (vertical bar).
:0	Displays the chord suffix selection dialog box where you can choose any suffix (colon zero).

Using Hidden Notes to put chords where there is no note to attach it to:

In the following example, there is a chord change every beat, but there are no notes on beats 2, 3, or 4 to attach the chord. Or are there?

Example 5.18a

By putting notes in other layers and then hiding them (you remember how to do that, don't you?) you can always put a chord anywhere you want. The example below is actually how to accomplish this.

Example 5.18b

Method #3: MIDI Input:

- With the Chord Tool selected, click "MIDI Input" under the Chord menu.
- Click on the note that you want to place a chord above.
- The "Ear" will appear signaling you to play your chord on your MIDI keyboard.
- Finale will determine what chord you played and ask you to learn the chord if it doesn't recognize it.

Exercise 5.19
Try this exercise using MIDI Input to enter the chords:

Method #4: One Staff Analysis
Method #5: Two Staff Analysis
Method #6: All Staff Analysis

Methods 4, 5, and 6 are very similar. All create chord symbols automatically by analyzing one, two, or all the staves in your score.

If Finale doesn't recognize a chord, it gives you the option of teaching it the chord or allowing it to guess the chord, which could produce some really wild chord spellings.

Exercise 5.20

- Enter the following chords.

- Then use the Chord Tool and switch to One Staff Analysis.

- Click on each chord for Finale to automatically add chords.

Exercise 5.21

- Enter the following two measures.

- Switch to the Chord Tool.

- First, try One Staff Analysis on each note in the top and bottom staff.

- Switch to the Two Staff Analysis and click only on each note in the top staff.

- Which chords are correct?

Exercise 5.22

- Now add the following bass line to the above two measures.

- Switch to the Chord Tool.

- Try All Staff Analysis on each note in the top staff.

- How is it different than the Two Staff Analysis?

More on Chord Styles:

Finale allows you to specify how you want your chords to be spelled using a variety of styles:

Standard: Finale displays the chord root and alternate bass note as letters. An accidental, if present, follows the chord root.

European: Finale displays the chord root and alternate bass note as letters. An accidental, if present, follows the chord root. This style is the same as Standard, with one exception; Finale always displays a natural sign on B natural.

German: Finale displays the chord root and alternate bass note as letters. An accidental, if present, follows the chord root. This style displays "es" for the flat sign and "is" for the sharp sign, with the following exceptions: E-flat is displayed as "Es"; A-flat is displayed as "As"; B-flat appears as B, and B appears as H.

Roman: Finale uses Roman numerals to represent the chord root and alternate bass note. An accidental, if present, precedes the chord root. When entering chords, type upper or lowercase letters to determine whether lower case Roman numerals are used. For example, in the key of C Major, C = I, d=ii, e=iii, F = IV, and so on.

Nashville A: Finale displays the chord root and alternate bass note as a scale degree number. An accidental, if present, **precedes** the chord root. In the key of C Major, 1 indicates a C chord, 2 indicates a D chord, 3 an E chord, and so on, up to 7, which indicates a B chord.

Nashville B: Finale displays the chord root and alternate bass note as a scale degree number. An accidental, if present, **follows** the chord root. In the key of C Major, 1 indicates a C chord, 2 indicates a D chord, 3 an E chord, and so on, up to 7, which indicates a B chord.

Solfeggio: Finale displays the chord root as Do, Di, Ra, Re, Ri and so on, starting with Do as the first scale degree, Di the next half-step, Re the second scale degree, and so on. As an example, the following table shows how Finale displays the chord root for each scale degree and half-step in the key of C Major.

Scandinavian: Finale displays the chord root and alternate bass note as letters. An accidental, if present, follows the chord root. This style is the same as Standard, with a few exceptions: instead of B♭, B and B♯ you get B♭, H and H♯.

Putting it all together:

Enter the following version of the Twelve Days of Christmas.

Things to keep in mind:

- Use the Repeat Tool for the endings. Remember, endings need a beginning and an ending repeat bracket.

- Carefully align the lines of the ending brackets and move them up and out of the way of the chords.

- Use the Chord Tool to enter the chords.

- Use the Lyric Tool to enter the lyrics. Change the current verse under the Lyric menu for verses 2-5.

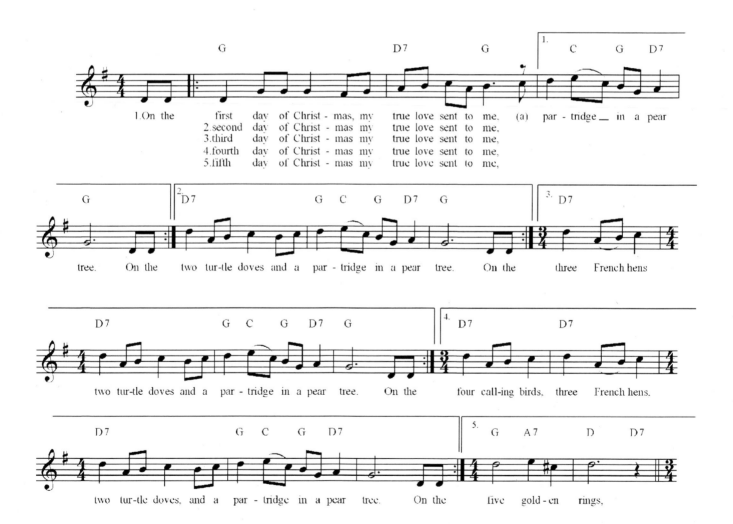

Tools covered in this chapter are listed below:

Selection Tool

Staff Tool

Resize Tool

Text Tool

Page Layout Tool

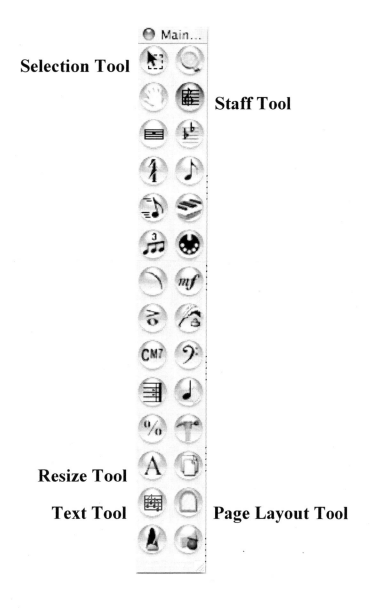

Scroll View vs. Page View

Up to now, all the work we have been doing has been in "Scroll View." You can think of Scroll View as just the first page of a score that is infinitely large. There are no page turns or ends of the page. You just "scroll" left, right, up or down to see more of the page. When you add more instruments or measures, you keep enlarging the page.

In "Page View" everything is finite. You must specify how large a page you want and page breaks are created accordingly. Page View is "WYSIWYG" or "What You See Is What You Get."

Example 6.1
Scroll View

Example 6.2
Page View

You can easily zoom in or out to display the entire page:

To view the entire page use "Fit in Window" (shown here):

View → Scale View to → Fit In Window.

Example 6.3
Page View Style

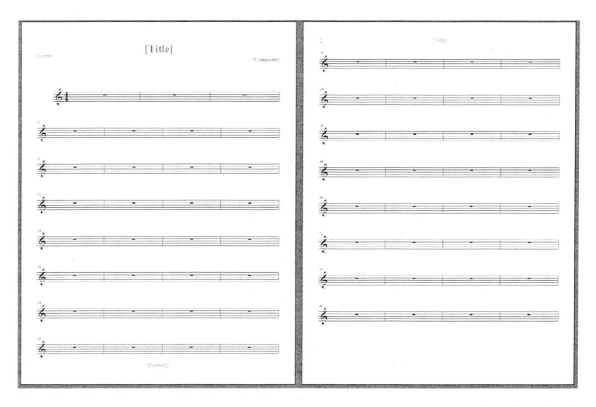

Page View Styles allow you to view more than one page in several different configurations:

Book Style: Row	Shows two pages at a time horizontally.
Book Style: Column	Shows two pages at a time vertically.
Book Style: Tiled	Tiled so a new row begins beneath the top row when the document window is not wide enough to fit all pages.
Book Style: Current Page Spread Only	Displays two pages at a time in Page View.
Loose-leaf Style: Row	Single (loose-leaf) pages horizontally.
Loose-leaf Style: Column	Single (loose-leaf) pages vertically.
Loose-leaf Style: Tiled	One page at a time, tiled so a new row begins beneath the top row when the document window is not wide enough to fit all pages.
Loose-leaf Style: Current Page Only	Displays one page at a time in Page View.

Resize Tool

This tool lets you reduce or enlarge a note, group of notes, staff, system, page, or all the music in a piece. When you use it at the note-by-note level, you can create cue notes; at the staff level, you can create a cue staff. You'll probably use this tool most often to reduce the overall size of the music.

Make sure that you have Automatic Update Layout selected. Otherwise, you will have to manually choose Update Layout from the Edit menu after you reduce a system, a page, or the entire piece so that Finale corrects any irregularities in measure widths introduced by the size change.

When the Resize Tool is selected and you click on a musical element, Finale displays the Resize dialog box where you can specify the amount of reduction or enlargement for that element. Depending on where you click, you will change the size of certain parts of the note, note head, staff, system, or page. See below:

 Special Mouse Clicks

- **Click directly on a notehead** to reduce/enlarge the notehead itself. (If the note is in Voice 2, shift-click it.)
- **Click a note stem** to reduce/enlarge the entire note, including the notehead, stem, flag, any other notes in the same chord, and - if the note you clicked was the first note of a beamed group - any other notes in the beamed group. (If the note is in Voice 2, shift-click.)
- **Click to the left of a staff** in Page View to reduce or enlarge the staff.
- **Click between and to the left of any two staves** in Page View to reduce or enlarge the entire system. (You must have two or more staves in the system).
- **Click the upper-left corner of a page in Page View**, to reduce or enlarge that page, a range of pages beginning with the one you clicked, or all pages from the one you clicked through the last page of the score.

Example 6.4

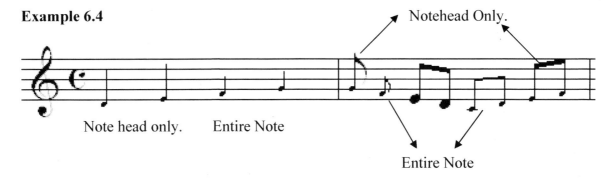

Notehead Only.

Note head only.   Entire Note

Entire Note

Resizing the Page

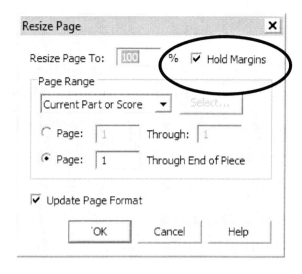

You can use Resize Page by clicking the upper left corner of the page in Page View.

Finale's 100% is a little bit too large for professional- looking parts. Most people use either 85% or 90%.

To fit your larger scores on letter or legal size paper, change the percentage until you can see all your parts clearly.

Hold Margins: When selected, the current page size is maintained and the music (and other elements) is resized. Otherwise the size of the page is resized by the specified amount.

Update Page Layout: When selected, the page resize setting in the Page Format for Score dialog box (Options menu) will be updated to match the resizing made here.

Example 6.5

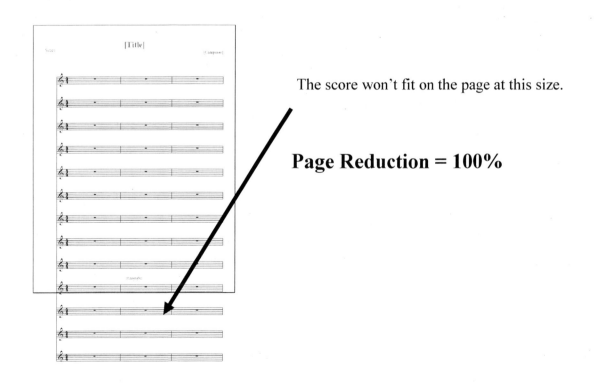

The score won't fit on the page at this size.

Page Reduction = 100%

Example 6.6

After resizing the page to 70% everything fits perfectly.

Page Reduction = 70%

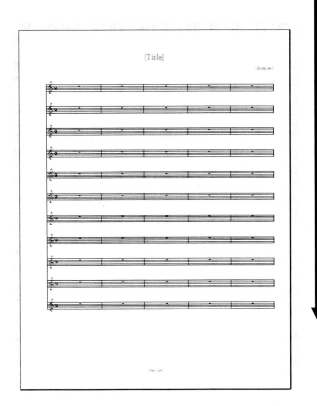

Text Tool

- The Text Tool allows you to place lines of text anywhere in your score. Text can span multiple lines and appear on one or more pages.

- With the Text Tool selected, double click anywhere in the score to create a new text block. Double-click drag to create a frame for the text.

- Use the Text Menu to change font, size, and appearance and to place inserts in your text such as sharps and flats.

Frame Attributes:

Frame Attributes allow you to place a text block on one or more pages. It also allows you to quickly position the text as a header or footer and align it left, right, or center.

Inserts:
Make your music look professional and use the proper musical symbols in your text blocks.

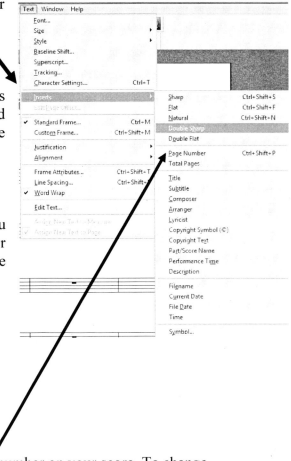

The inserts submenu contains shortcuts for such things as sharps and flats as well as the Title, Composer, and Arranger information you may have entered during the Document Setup Wizard process.

You will also use the "Part/Score Name" insert if you use linked parts. This insert should be used in a header in the score. It will then display either "Score" or the actual instrument name needed when printing parts.

Page Numbers:
Use Text → Inserts → Page Number to place a page number on your score. To change the page number on a page, you must use "Edit Page Offset." Change the Page Offset to <u>one less</u> than what you want the actual page number to be (n-1).

Finale for Composers

102

Example 6.7

Use the Text Tool to create all the text in the following example:

You can also use the text tool to put long blocks of text into your score.

Just remember if you put it in the scroll view you won't be able to edit it then page view. So be careful and plan what you need to accomplish with the text and if it needs to be printed on the players part.

Symphony No. 1 in B♭

Dedicated to the very hard working students of the Wednesday night
Finale Class at Carnegie Mellon University.

Composer

- 10 -

Finale for Composers

Page Layout Tool

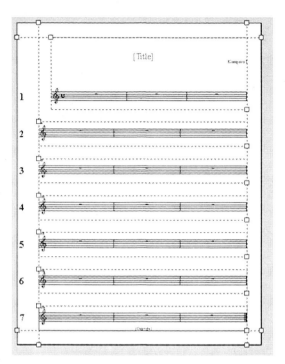

This tool lets you define the page layout for your score, including the page size, size of the page margins, and the positioning of the systems on each page.

The screen changes to Page Layout View when you click the Page Layout Tool. In this view, you can change the page size, margins, or system positioning, either one page at a time or for the entire score at once.

The Page Layout menu contains a command for optimizing systems (hiding empty staves within each system to produce a more compact and readable full score), and another for fitting measures on a line, so that you can specify the number of measures you want on each line of music.

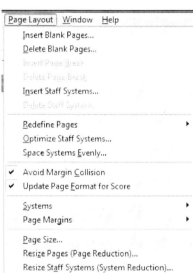

Changing Page Size:

- Select "Page Size…" from the Page Layout Menu.
- Change the values for your page size.
- Select either the current page, all pages, left pages, right pages, or a page range to be changed.

Changing Page Margins:

- Select "Page Margins→ Edit Page Margins" from the Page Layout Menu.
- Change the values for the margins.
- Select the current page, all pages, left pages, right pages, or a page range to be changed.

OR

- Select "Page Margins →" and the type of change you want to make-- current page, all pages, left pages, right pages, or a page range.
- Move the little boxes on the page layouts to create the margins you want.

Changing Staff Systems:

- Select "Systems → Edit Margins" from the Page Layout Menu.
- Click on which system you want to edit (For the whole score, click on the first system).
- Change the values for the system margins.
- Select the range of systems you want or click the "All Systems" button.
- Click Apply.
- Click Close.

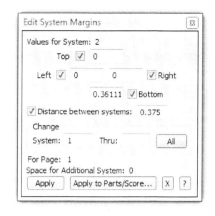

IMPORTANT CONSIDERATIONS:

Changing Staff Systems:

<u>To make more staves fit on a page</u>: Drag the first staff **UP** while in Edit System Margins, select All Systems, then select "Apply."

<u>To make more room between all staves</u>: Drag the first staff **DOWN** while in Edit System Margins, select "All Systems", then select "Apply."

To make all staves look like the first system: Select "All Systems" while in Edit System Margins, the click "Apply."

Example 6.8

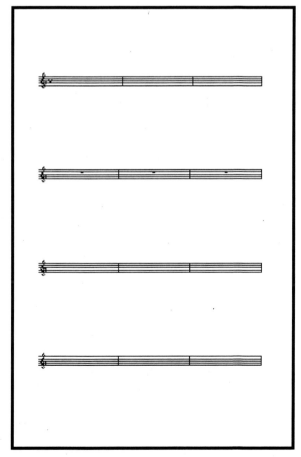

Try this example:

- Set your score pages to legal size (8.5" x 14")

- Adjust the staff systems so that only 4 fit on the page as in the picture at the left.

Other Page Layout Options:

When the Page Layout Tool is selected, you have several other utilities under the Page Layout Menu:

- **<u>Insert Blank Pages:</u>**
  Use this dialog box to insert blank pages **<u>(pages that do not contain music but can contain text blocks)</u>** at any point in your score.

- **<u>Delete Blank Pages:</u>**
  Choose this command to display the Delete Blank Pages dialog box in which you can delete blank pages in your score.

- **<u>Insert Page Break:</u>**
  Click on a system to select it and then select Insert Page Break to start a new page starting with the system you selected.

- **<u>Delete Page Break:</u>**
  Click on a system to select it and then select Delete Page Break to remove the page break you created.

- **<u>Insert Staff Systems:</u>**
  Click on a system to select it and then select Insert Staff Systems. You then can create a new system without disturbing the surrounding music.

- **<u>Delete Staff Systems:</u>**
  Deletes the selected system without disturbing the surrounding music.

- **<u>Redefine Pages:</u>**
  Use this command to redefine the pages in the score back to the settings in the Page Format for Score dialog box. **This command removes all formatting so use with caution.**

- **<u>Optimize Staff Systems:</u>**
  Hides empty staves within each system. **Optimizing has another important benefit**: it permits staves to be independently movable in Page View. Under normal circumstances, you can only move, respace, or rearrange staves for all systems using the Staff Tool. If you have optimized a system however, you'll find that the Staff Tool works in Page View as well, letting you vary the positioning and spacing of staves as they'll appear on the printed page. Furthermore, again using the Staff Tool, you can change the staff grouping of staves that have been optimized, letting you change the way in which your staves are bracketed.

- **<u>Space Systems Evenly:</u>**
  Moves the systems so they are evenly spaced between the top and bottom margins of the page. Specify which pages to space evenly, whether to allow systems to move from one page to another, and when to skip spacing a partially-empty page.

Exercise 6.9

Blank Page Exercise:
- Create about 100 measures of music.
- Switch to Page Layout.
- Insert a blank page at the beginning of your score.
- Put some kind of text on the page, like a header or footer, for example, using the Text Tool.
- Switch to the second page to see that the music starts there.
- Delete the blank page with the Page Layout Menu Option.
- See that the music now starts on the first page again.

This is a blank page for text, titles or good page turns.

Exercise 6.10
Optimized Staff Systems Example:
- Create about 30 measures of music in one staff.
- Create 2 other staves, but leave them blank.
- Make a Group containing all 3 staves.
- Switch to Page View.
- Select the Page Layout Tool and select Page Layout→Optimize Staff Systems.
- Click [OK].
- Check to see if you are left with one only staff system.
- Remove the optimization:
- Select the Page Layout Tool and select Page Layout→Optimize Staff Systems.
- Click Remove Staff system Optimization.
- Click [OK].

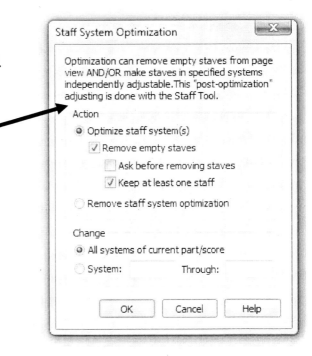

BEFORE OPTIMIZATION: **AFTER OPTIMIZATION:**

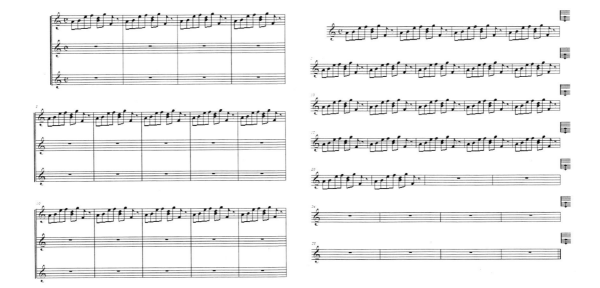

Exercise 6.11
Grouping/Moving Measures One at a Time:

Instead of grouping your whole score in the same number of measures, it is often better to move measures one at a time near where you need more or less space. Use the Selection Tool and the Up and Down cursor keys to move the measure.

- Create about 100 measures of music in one staff.
- Switch to Page View.
- Select the Selection Tool (or any tool that allows you to select an entire measure) and click on a measure you want to either move to the previous system or the next system.
- Press the [UP ARROW] to move the measure to the system above.
- Press the [DOWN ARROW] to move the measure to the system below.

Click this measure with the Selection Tool and then press the UP ARROW on the keyboard to force it on the previous system as shown below:

The little locks ⌂ **denote that you forced or "locked" the measures in the current configuration.**

Exercise 6.12
Grouping/Moving Measures by Selection:

You can group several measures on one line by selecting them with the Selection Tool and clicking Utilities →Fit Measures.

- Create about 100 measures of music in one staff.

- Switch to Page View.

- Select the Selection Tool and select Utilities →Fit Music.

- Type "3" and click [OK].

- Check to see if the music now has 3 measures per system.

- Select the Page Layout Tool and select Page Layout→Fit Music.

- Type "1" and click [OK]. Check to see if the music now has 1 long measure per system.

Fit to 3 Measures per System

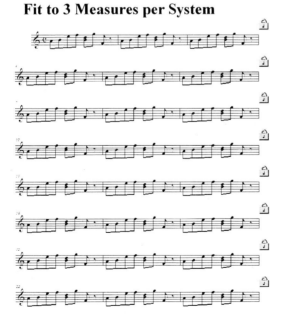

Fit to 1 Measure per System

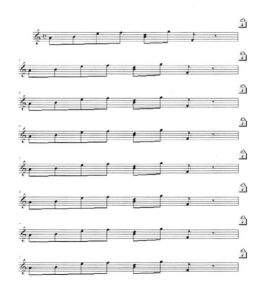

- Select several measures that are on two different systems by dragging the selection around them or shift clicking on them.
- Click Utilities → Fit Measures.
- Click "Lock Selected Measures into One System."
- Click [OK].
- All the selected measures should now be on one staff. (You can see that the measures are locked together by the lock on the right side of the staff.)
- Remove the lock by either using "Remove System Locks" or Unlock measures with the Selection Tool and Utilities → Unlock Systems.

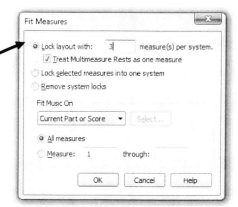

These selected measures will be locked into one system as shown below:

If you don't see the locks, make sure "Show Page Layout Icons" is selected under the View Menu.

Page Format for Score

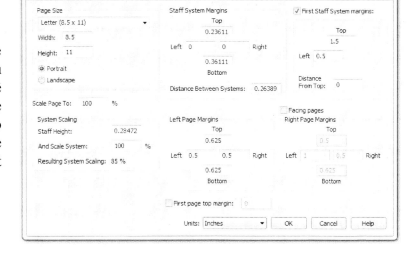

Page Format for Score under the Document Menu is where you define the default setup for score pages. This is also where the values come from when you do "Redefine Pages" with the Page Layout Tool, i.e., the pages get redefined to the values set here.

Below are the various options and their uses:

- **Page Size: Height • Width • Portrait • Landscape.**

- **System Scaling: Staff Height • And Scale System • Resulting System Scaling.** Set the staff height, then apply a percentage to the value. The Resulting System Scaling is the cumulative effect for all staves in the score (in other words, the staff height you specify will be further adjusted by the system percentage).

- **Scale Page to:** You can change the number in this text box to specify the percentage of enlargement or reduction you want to apply to the music on all pages, expressed as a percentage of normal size.

- **Staff System Margins: Top • Left • Bottom • Right • Distance Between Systems.** The System Margins represent the distance from the edge of each system to the Page margins (Right and Left), or the distance between one system and the one above it (Top), or the extra space between the bottom of one system and the top of the next (Bottom). The distance between the bottom of one system and top of the following system is the distance between systems.

- **First Staff System Margins: Top • Left • Distance from Top.** Use these controls to make room for the title on the first page of your score. Enter a value in the Top text box to tell Finale how far down the page to place the first system, measured from the top page margin. The Left value specifies how far you want Finale to indent the first system on the first page. Enter a value for the distance from the page margin.

- **Left Page Margins: Top • Bottom • Left • Right.** The settings in this group box apply to newly created left pages when you've selected Facing Pages. All even-numbered pages are considered Left pages (as Finale numbers them in Page View). When Facing Pages is not selected, these settings apply to all newly created pages.

- **Facing Pages.** When this checkbox is selected, Finale automatically uses the settings in both the Left and Right Page Margins group boxes for new left and right pages in your score. Select this option if you want different formats or margins for your left and right pages. To Finale, all even pages are left-facing pages, and all odd pages are right-facing pages (as Finale numbers them at the bottom of the window in Page View). If Facing Pages is not selected, Finale uses the Left Page Margins settings for every page.

- **Right Page Margins: Top • Bottom • Left • Right.** These settings apply to newly created right pages when Facing Pages is selected. All odd-numbered pages are considered right pages (as Finale numbers them in Page View). When Facing Pages is not selected, Finale does not use these settings.

- **First Page Top Margin.** Check this box to use a different value for the first page from the default for other pages. This value sets the position of the top page margin on the first page of your music. Enter a value to specify where, measured from the top of the page, Finale should place the music.

Page Setup & Printing

Page Setup...
IMPORTANT:
The changes you make here <u>do not affect the format of the score</u>. These settings only affect the printer and paper selection. In almost all cases these settings should match the settings you make with the Page Layout Tool. If not, unpredictable results will occur.

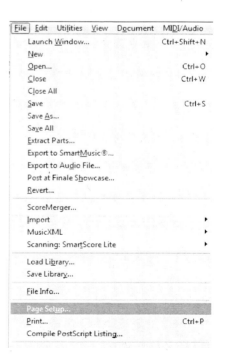

Printing the Score...

Select File→ Print... to print your score as it appears in Page View. This will allow you to print your score, parts, or any combination thereof. The contents of this dialog box vary slightly according to the printer and print driver used with your computer.

For now, you will only have the choice to print your score. Other options deal mostly with printer setting such as printing in color or printing crop marks and how many pages to print per page.

Putting it all together...

Try to print the score to this excerpt of the Haydn String Quartet in G Major:

Chapter 7
Creating Perfect Parts

Tools covered in this chapter are listed below:

Selection Tool

Measure Tool

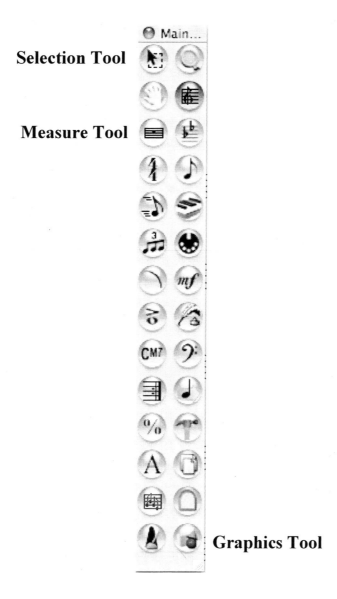

Graphics Tool

Printing Parts

In early versions of Finale, there were two ways to print your parts: from the now obsolete "Print Parts" command under the File menu and by extracting and formatting the parts as separate files. Fortunately, those days are gone and Finale now creates what are called "Linked Parts"—parts that stayed linked to the score and are saved in the score file. The main advantage of this is that you no longer have to maintain a file for the score and one for each of the parts. Without linked parts, after you had extracted all the parts and found a mistake or wanted to make a change in the score, you had to edit the score file and all of the affected parts files. Now when you make a change in the score, all the linked parts are changed as well.

Linked parts also make printing much easier. Using the old "Print Parts..." command produced unprofessional (and largely unusable part) as shown below. If you did extract each part and formatted it, printing all those separate files turned into a real nightmare. Now with linked parts, you can easily select which parts you want to print, and those will all be printed with one simple command.

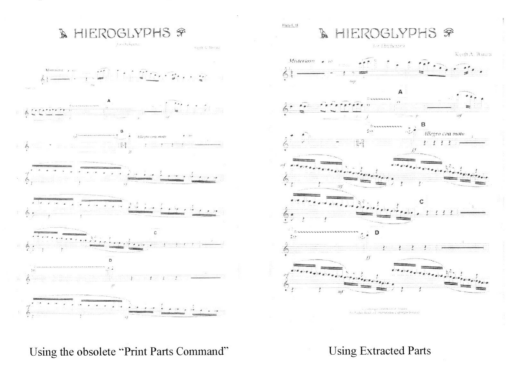

Using the obsolete "Print Parts Command"   Using Extracted Parts

You can still export separate files for parts using the "Extract Parts..." command, however you will most likely want to try to use linked parts whenever possible. The only real use for extracted parts I can think of is if you would want to send separate Finale files to a client, for example. However, you can easily create separate PDF files using linked files.

Creating Linked Parts

To begin the process of creating linked parts, select "Manage Parts…" under the document menu.

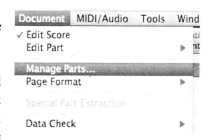

Depending on whether you used the Document Setup Wizard or created your score by hand, you may not see any linked parts in the Manage Parts windows. If that's the case, you can easily create a part for each staff in your score by clicking the "Generate Parts" button.

If you want to see or change which staves are in each part, click the "Edit Part Definition >>" button. Here you can add or remove staves to each part. For example, perhaps you want to put all of the percussion staves on one part. This can be done by selecting the instrument name on the right and then clicking "Add to part." You can also change the order of the instruments on the part by clicking on the instrument under "Staves and groups in part" and then clicking "move up" or "move down."

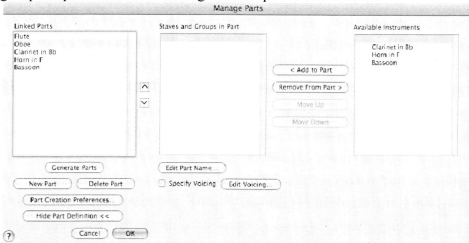

You can specify what type of music spacing to apply to each part, if you want to create multi-measure rests, and set the page format for the parts by first clicking "Part Creation Preferences…" and then selecting the appropriate options.

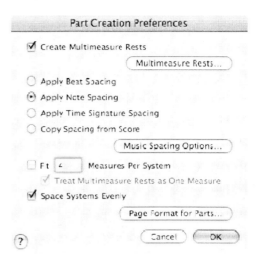

I would not change the music spacing option to "Copy Spacing from Score." This would have the effect of making the music spacing of the part the same as in the score. Since the score spacing is dependent on the spacing all of the instruments vertically in the score, measures need to be large enough to accommodate all instruments. In an individual part, you most often only have the music spacing of one staff to worry about. It therefore would look very odd to use the music spacing of the score.

You can also fit *x* number of measures per line of music or space systems evenly on the page so that each system has the same amount of space as the one above and below it does.

Editing Linked Parts

Now that you have created your linked parts, it's time to make any part specific edits you want to make. To edit parts, select "Edit Part" from the Document menu, then select the part you want to edit.

You will then only be able to see and edit the part you selected. If you want to go back to the score, select "Edit Score" from the Document menu. Any time you make a change to the part, such as moving a dynamic or tempo marking, the item will change color to denote that it has been modified from the position it had in the score. If you want to restore it to its original position, right click or control-click and select "Re-link to Score."

What items might you want to take a look at in each part before printing?
- Page Turns: Make sure there is enough time for the player to turn the page. Move measures to the next system and systems to the next page to accomplish this.
- Make sure all markings are not touching notes or other symbols. Occasionally you might have to place dynamics or expressions in the score, in non-ideal locations so that they will fit among other staves. Now is the time to clean them up in the part so that they can be easily read.
- Headers/Footers: Make sure that headers such as title and composer are positioned appropriately. These often need to be moved from their position in the score.
- Page numbers: Make sure these are in the correct location on each page.
- Instrument Names: It is good practice to put the instrument name on each page of the part. How do you do this? Create a header using the "Score/Part Name" insert. See Chapter 6 for complete details.

"Extracted" Parts

If you still want to extract parts instead of using Linked Parts or have the need for separate Finale files for each part, here are some tips for extracting the parts. It is important to remember that Finale uses all of the modifications you made in editing parts when it extracts them to separate files.

Steps for Extracting Parts:

1. Make a copy of your score file (so you will have a clean copy when you want to print the score).
2. Generate the parts as shown earlier in this chapter. NOTE: If you do not have any parts generated, you will not be able to extract any.
3. Make any editing or formatting changes as described earlier in this chapter.
4. Chose "Extract Parts" under the File menu.
5. Select Parts that you want to extract. Remember to set up parts with two staves such as piano in the Manage Parts window.

6. Click OK to extract your parts. New file names can be automatically generated by specifying the variables you wish to use in the file name. For example, "%f %s" would yield a file name of the "file name of your **score**" plus and "the **staff name** of the part." Or, you can have Finale prompt you for each part name. Just remember what part Finale is extracting before you type in a name.
7. When Finale has completed all the part extractions, open each part individually and inspect for proper spacing of dynamics, articulations, slurs, text, page numbers, etc. This step is what makes your parts look professional. The more time you take here to "clean up" any stray symbols, the better your parts will look.
8. **Page Turns!!!** If you didn't work out the page turns when you edited the linked part in Finale, you must rework the pages now.
9. Save the part with the proper name if Finale didn't already do so.

Words of Wisdom:

In the first edition of *Finale for Composers,* I said that extracted parts were the only acceptable process if you wanted to create professional looking parts. Now, with newer versions of Finale offering linked parts, I see no for extracting the parts. Only in rare cases where you would want to do major formatting changes to the parts that would disrupt the score, would I see any need for extracting the parts. As mentioned earlier, it is so much more convenient to have all of the parts in one file and even easier when it is time to print them. So spend some time getting used to linked parts. I am sure you will grow to love them.

Graphics Tool

The Graphics Tool is used to import and export graphics from Finale. You can bring in outside graphics files for use within Finale as well as export a region of music or even pages of music as EPS or TIFF files. These files can then be used in other applications such as word processors or desktop publishing software.

In newer versions of Finale, the Graphics Tool is found under the Advanced Tool Palette.

Update Note:

In earlier versions, Finale didn't actually save imported graphic files in your Finale document. In more current versions, you now have the option to embed the graphic file in the document. Now this is the default behavior. So as long as you embed the file, you can delete it from your storage drive.

Options for the Graphics Tool are found under the Graphics Menu when the tool is selected:

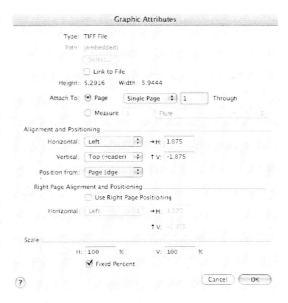

Place Graphic…:
Imports a graphic into your score. You can specify what page(s) to show it on, or what measure it is attached to and its position, by double clicking on the image (see right).

Export Pages:
Allows you to save an image of the music to use in another program. Select "Export Pages" from the Graphics menu and specify in which pages and in what format you want them exported.

Export Selection:
Allows you export a section of the music. **IMPORTANT**: You must **Double click and drag** the selection rectangle around the portion of music you want to export. Then select "Export Selection" from the Graphics menu.

Check Graphics:
Checks to see if the links to the graphics in your score are valid, i.e. there are no missing graphic files. This option is only useful if you choose not to embed your graphic files. In that case, Finale would create a link to the file on your storage drive. This command checks to see if that link is still valid.

Exercise 7.1
Shape in Score Exercise:

- Find a graphic on your hard drive or some other location.
- Switch to Page View.
- With the graphic tool selected, choose "Place Graphic" and place the picture on the first page of your score.
- Make sure that the graphic only appears on the first page.

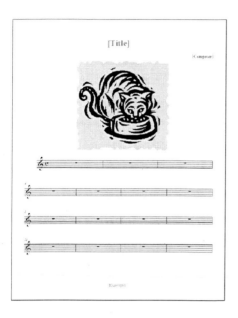

Graphics can also be imported into the Shape Editor to become part of your custom shape. Click on the small shape graphics tool icon when you are in the Shape Editor to import your graphic.

Exercise 7.2
Graphic Imported into Expression Exercise:

- Make a new shape with the Expression tool.
- Insert your graphic file into the shape editor by clicking the small graphic tool icon and clicking the shape edit window.
- Hit "OK" and "Select" several times until you exit the shape designer.
- Place the shape in a measure of your score.

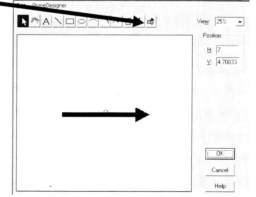

Special Mouse Clicks

- Click in the Shape Designer display area to place a graphic in the Shape Designer. The Open dialog box appears displaying the available EPS, PICT and TIFF graphics.
- Click a graphic or drag-enclose graphics to select a graphic or graphics. Eight bounding handles appear on each selected graphic.
- Shift-click a graphic Add a graphic to the selection. If a graphic is already selected, remove the graphic from the selection.
- Double-click a graphic to edit the graphic's attributes. The Graphic Attributes dialog box appears.
- Double-click in the score to place a graphic in the score. The Open dialog box appears displaying the available EPS, PICT and TIFF graphics.
- Double-click and drag to enclose a region in Page View Select a region containing the musical example to export.
- Press delete for one or more selected graphics to delete the selected graphics.
- Drag a selected graphic to adjust the graphic's position in the score.
- Drag a graphic's bounding handle to resize the graphic horizontally or vertically

UPDATE LAYOUT:

To speed up operations, Finale does not constantly recalculate the positioning and page layout of measures within your score. Instead, this recalculation only takes place when you request it by choosing Update Layout from the Edit menu.

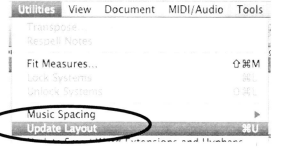

When you choose this command, Finale uses the settings in the Update Layout Options dialog box to determine what parts of the music layout it will recalculate to reflect the changes in positioning and page layout.

When would you need to use Update Layout? If your music looks strange in Page View or if you made a change in the size of the music that didn't affect the spacing of music as shown in the following example.

Here is the original music at 100%:

Now change the size of the music with the Resize tool to 50%:

Notice how the notes are smaller but the number of measures per line does not change after you change the Page Percent.

After Selecting Update Layout:

Once Update Layout is selected, you can see that the number of measures per line has also increased.

SPECIAL PART EXTRACTION:

This command provides access to one of Finale's three-part-printing methods. Using Special Part Extraction, you can see the full score in Scroll View, while the extracted part appears, ready for editing and printing in Page View.

Exercise 7.6

To use Special Part Extraction:

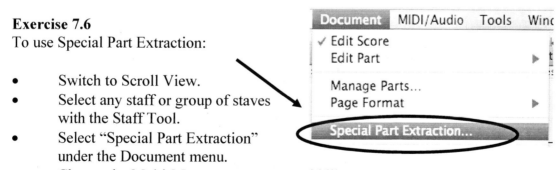

- Switch to Scroll View.
- Select any staff or group of staves with the Staff Tool.
- Select "Special Part Extraction" under the Document menu.
- Choose the Multi-Measure rest you would like to use.
- Click "OK".
- Switch to Page View to see the special part you just made.

Scroll View- Full Score   **Page View-Special Part Extraction**

Update Note:

In earlier versions, Finale didn't have Linked Parts, and Special Part Extraction was the only way to create parts in Finale with two or more staves. With the advent of linked parts where you can create parts using any combination of staves, Special Part Extraction is rarely used anymore.

Creating & Splitting Multi-Measure Rests

To manually create a multi-measure rest:

When you create parts using Linked Parts or Special Part Extraction, Finale groups all empty measures into multi-measure rests. If you would rather control which measures get combined into multi-measure rests, you can manually select the measures you want to combine into a multi-measure rest in your score.

- **Click the Selection Tool, the Measure Tool, or any tool that allows you to select a group of measures**.
- **Select the region that contains the measures you want to display as a multi-measure rest.** You can also select your whole score. (You must be in Page View to do this.)
- **Choose Multi-Measure Rests → Create from the Edit Menu.**

Exercise 7.7

Finale creates multi-measure rests in the selected region, using the same rules as when it automatically creates them in Linked Parts or Special Part Extraction to create rests—breaking them at key and time signatures, or when you've selected Break a Multi-Measure Rest in the Measure Attributes dialog box for the measure or when an Expression is assigned to do so.

IMPORTANT: In order for measures to be grouped, they must contain default whole rests. If a whole rest was manually entered in a measure, that measure will not be included in a multi-measure rest until you erase the whole rest (using the Simple Entry or Speedy Entry tools, or the Selection Tool's Clear command).

You can also use old style symbols instead of a multi-measure rest shape. Select "Use Symbols for rests less than _____ Measures."

Example 7.8

3 measures

7 measures

9 measures

To break a multi-measure rest

There may be times when you want to break a large multi-measure rest into two or more smaller groups. Here's how:

- **Click the Selection Tool,** the Measure Tool or any tool that allows you to select more than one measure.
- **Select the multi-measure** rest to break. To break more than one multi-measure rest, select a region that contains the rests. (Remember that you must be in Page View to do this.)
- **Choose Multi-Measure Rests → Break from the Edit menu.** Finale breaks the multi-measure rests in the selected region into separate measures of rests. You can then reverse the process by selecting only the measures you want to group and create a multi-measure rest.

Example 7.10:

Before:

After Breaking a Multi-Measure Rest:

To edit the appearance of a multi-measure rest

You can also edit the appearance of any single multi-measure rest. If more than one multi-measure rest is selected, Finale changes only the first rest in the region.

Note: If you find that you're using the Edit command frequently to change rests, consider changing the global settings in the Options Menu. See "To set up the appearance of multi-measure rests."

- **Click the Selection Tool,** the Measure Tool or any tool that allows you to select more than one measure.
- **Select the multi-measure** rest you want to change. (You must be in Page View to do this).
- **Choose Multi-Measure Rests → Edit from the Edit Menu.**
- **Specify the settings** you want Finale to use for this multi-measure rest.
- **Click OK** to return to the score where Finale displays your new settings.
- **Optional: Choose Update Layout** from the Edit Menu to ensure that Finale is displaying the current layout of the score.

Example 7.11:

BEFORE:

AFTER:

The above example is a common edit you may need to make when dealing with multi-measure rests positioned near clef changes. By changing the ending point of the multi-measure rest to -0.1, the multi-measure rest is now separated from the clef. (Note that this behavior has been corrected in more recent versions of Finale).

Exercise 7.12:

To display a measure number range for a multi-measure rest

- **Click the Measure Tool** 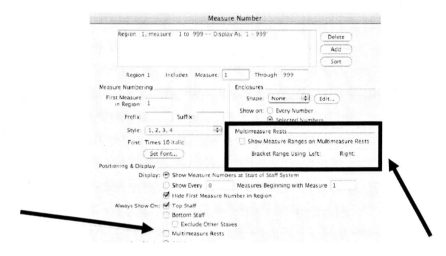.

- **Choose Edit Measure Number Regions... from the Measure Menu.**

- **Click Show Measure Number Ranges on Multi-Measure Rests.** You can also specify a symbol to bracket the left and right range such as "[   ]".

- Additionally, you can click "Always Show on Multi-Measure Rests" to force measure number ranges to appear on all multi-measure rests.

- **If your measure number is not displayed, choose Show Number from the Measure Numbers submenu of the Measure Menu.** If the current multi-measure rest is not designated to show in the current measure number region, "Show" must be forced on. If you always want to show ranges, click "Always Show on Multi-Measure Rests" as described above.

Putting it all together...

Creating Parts Exercise:

- Enter the following short excerpt.
- Format and Print the completed score.
- Generate linked parts and format each one.
- Print each part.

QUARTET NO. 57
In G Major

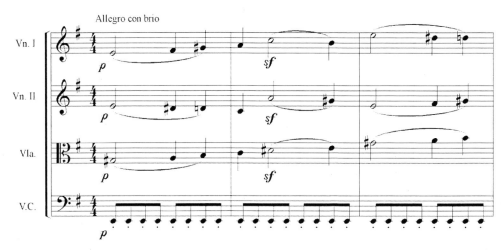

Tools covered in this chapter are listed below:

Selection Tool 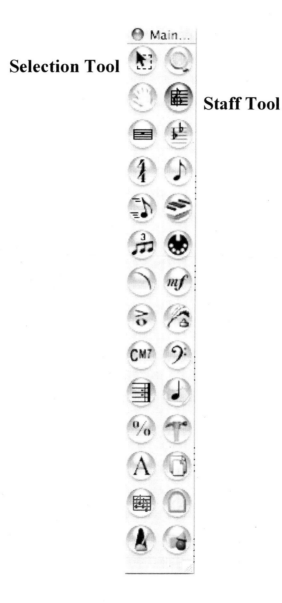 Staff Tool

Selection Tool: Copy and Paste Functions

One of the most common uses for the Selection tool is to copy and paste music in your score.

Example 8.1

To Copy a complete measure using the Selection tool, click on the measure and DRAG it to where you want it copied.

- Click the Selection Tool.
- Click on the measure from which you want to copy.
- Drag the measure with the music one measure to the right.
- Note: the music is pasted at the beat to which you drag it. The measure will be outlined in green when you are pasting it to the first beat of the measure.
- If you are copying more than one measure, make sure to drag the first measure in your selection to where you want the copy to start.
- You can also use the cut, copy, insert, and replace entries from under the Edit menu to perform similar functions.

Erasing Measures:
- Click on the measure(s) with the Selection Tool that you want to ERASE.
- Erasing clears all music and symbols from the selected measure but does not delete the measure.
- Hit Clear (MAC) or Backspace (PC) to Erase or select "Clear All Items" from the Edit menu.

Finale Terminology:

Measure Stack: A Measure Stack is all the measures above and below the selected measure(s). In other words, the stack contacts the measure or measures you have selected in all instruments/staves.

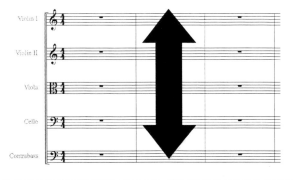

Deleting Measures:

- Click on the measure(s) with the Selection Tool that you want to DELETE.
- Select "Delete Measure Stack" from the Edit Menu.

Inserting Measures:

- Click on the measure(s) with the Selection Tool that you want to insert in a measure or measures BEFORE.
- Select "Insert Measure Stack…" from the Edit Menu.
- Specify how many measures to insert.

Select Region:

Sometimes the measures you want to copy or erase are not all on the screen. Select Region (under the Edit menu) allows you to easily and quickly select a large area of your score. Just enter the starting and ending staff, measure and even beat or EDU and the Selection Tool will select the encompassing area.

Filtered Copy and Paste:

There may be times when you want to copy only certain elements of your music such as only the notes or only the articulations. This can be easily accomplished using the "Filter" command found under the Edit Menu.

Setting up the Filter:

With this dialog box, you have the option of excluding some of the score elements— lyrics or expression, for example. The items in the filter let you specify which elements of the music you want to be placed on the Clipboard (ready for pasting elsewhere in the score).

Using the Filter:

Once you have specified filter settings, turn on the filter by selecting "Use Filter" under the Edit Menu.

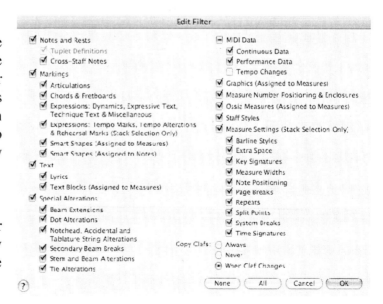

Exercise 8.2
Copy only the notes to the second measure using the Filter:

- Select "Edit Filter…" under the Edit Menu.
- Turn off everything except Notes and Rests. (Click "None" to turn everything off, the click "Notes and Rests" to turn it on).
- Turn on Filter by selecting "Use Filter" under the edit menu.
- Selection Tool selected, highlight the first measure.
- Copy the first measure and paste it into the second measure.
- Only the notes should have been copied if you did this function correctly.

Exercise 8.3

Turn off the Notes and Rests using the Filter. Then copy the first measure to the next two measures and see what happens.

Filtering On the Fly:
- Copy a measure or measures.
- Click in the measure where you want to place the music.
- Hold down Shift and select either "Insert and Filter" or "Paste and Filter" from the Edit Menu.
  - Insert and filters creates a new measure stack from the copied music.
  - Paste and Filter replaces the music with the copied music.
- The Edit Filter window will appear and allow you to choose what to copy.

Save to Clip File
You can also save the selected items to a clip file which you can then save to your storage drive for later use. Hold down CTRL on PC's or Option on Mac's and select Edit→Cut/Copy to Clip File… You will be prompted to name your clip file.

To import entries from a clip file, hold down CTRL on PC's or Option on Mac's and select Edit→ Insert/Replace Entries from Clip File… You will then be prompted to locate the clip file on your hard drive.

Edit	Utilities	View	Document
Undo Mass Insert			⌘Z
Can't Redo			⌘Y
Undo/Redo Lists…			⇧⌘Z
Select All			⌘A
Select Region…			
Cut to Clip File…			⌥⌘X
Copy to Clip File…			⌥⌘C
Insert From Clip File…			⌥⌘I
Paste From Clip File…			⌥⌘V
Paste Multiple…			^⌘V

Clearing Music

You saw on the previous pages how to copy certain items. You can also erase or clear certain items. You may, for example, want to clear only the lyrics in a certain passage, or the articulations or any special modifications you made to the notes use the Special Tools (see chapter 9).

Clearing with the Selection Tool Functions two ways:

- Clear All Items: Erases everything in the selected measure(s) Functions the same way as using the Clear key (Mac) or Backspace (PC).

- Clear Selected Items: Erases only the music items that you specify. This is useful for erasing chords, articulations, slurs, etc.

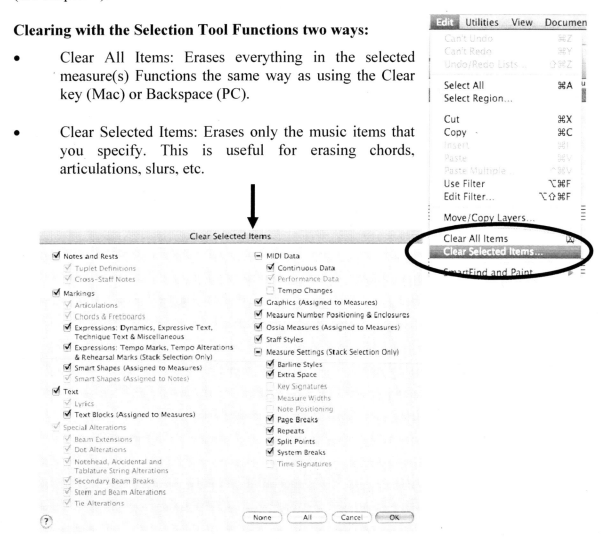

SmartFind and Paint

If you have rhythmically similar passages with the same articulations or phrasing, you can use Smart Find and Paint to quickly search your music and "paint" the corresponding symbols.

Exercise 8.4

Start with an example similar to this one containing rhythmically similar measures unto which you want to paint articulations and phrasings.

Then select the entire first measure with the Selection Tool and choose SmartFind and Paint → Set SmartFind Source Region from under the Edit menu. The measure you set as the source will then have a dark rectangle around it as shown below:

Choose SmartFind and Paint → Apply SmartFind and Paint... from under the Edit Menu. You then can choose which items to paint such as Slurs, Articulations, Smart Shapes, and Expressions.

If you want to search your entire piece, click "Paint All" and your music should look similar to this:

Or you can click "find," to search for the first instance of the source measure. If you want to paint the measure found, click "Paint" or click "Find" again to search for the next matching measure.

To stop searching, click SmartFind and Paint → Deselect SmartFind Source Region.

Utilities Menu

After selecting a measure or part of a measure with a tool such as the Selection Tool, you can chose any of the items under the Utlities Menu to further modify your music.

Transposing Music Measure by Measure

While you can set up your score so that the proper transposition is automatically done for each staff, there are times when you might need to transpose a few measures, perhaps for an oboe part that switches to English horn, or to add intervals to existing notes.

Diatonically:
Moves the notes up or down without regard to pitch or key.

Chromatically:
Move the notes up or down by the exact interval.

Preserve Original Notes:
Keeps the notes and **adds** notes at the specified intervals.

Exercise 8.5

Add octaves below: *Transpose down a third:*   *Add minor sixths below:*

Respell Notes:
Re-transcribes the pitches of the selected notes so they appear as they would have when entered for the first time.

Rebar & Rebeam Music

Rebar Music takes the selected measures and moves all the notes together according to the time signature. If you change the note values to larger or smaller values, more or fewer notes will fit in a measure. Rebar Music will fix the problem.

Example 8.6

←   Before   →   After:

There are also Rebar Options which allow you to specify where the rebarring should stop:
- End of Region Selected.
- Key Signature Changes.
- Time Signature Changes.
- Special Barlines or Repeats.
- Empty Measures.

This option also gives you the ability (which is on by default) of rebeaming your music. This is a good idea considering that notes will more than likely be moving to other measures and will need to be beamed properly in relation to the other notes next to them.

Rebeaming is very useful with you wish to beam your music to another time signature or to correct beaming mistakes when the notes were entered. Rebeam Music has three options:

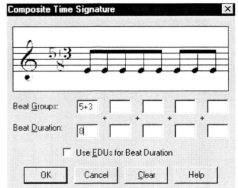

- **Rebeam Music:** Rebeams the music back to the original beaming that Finale created when the notes were first entered. This is based on the time signature of the music and will override any changes you may have manually done to change the default beaming.

- **Rebeam to Time Signature**: Allows you to specify how to beam the music by selecting or creating a time signature. You could beam a measure in 4/4 to 6/8 for example. This does <u>NOT </u>change the measure's time signature, but only the way the music is beamed. By using a "Composite Time Signature" you can create unique beamings while still using traditional time signatures. Since this changes only how the beams occur, it is useful for beaming 5/8 in groups of 5 notes as shown below when beamed to a composite time signature of 5+*anything*/8:

Example 8.7
Original   **Beamed to Time Signature of 5+3/8**

- **Rebeam to Lyrics**: Changes the beaming to break at each syllable as in traditional choral music. Also gives you an option to break at each beat.

Example 8.8

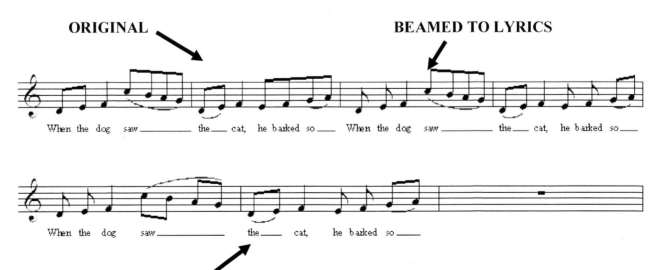

BEAMED TO LYRICS + BEAMED TO BEATS

Explode Music:

Breaks a chordal passage into individual, single-line melodies on separate staves.

THIS

BECOMES

THIS

Implode Music:

Condenses the music on the selected staves onto a single staff. (The opposite of "Explode Music.") Good for piano reductions.

SmartMusic® Markers

Allows you to add SmartMusic® markers to your music by selecting a measure and then choosing what type of marker you want to add.

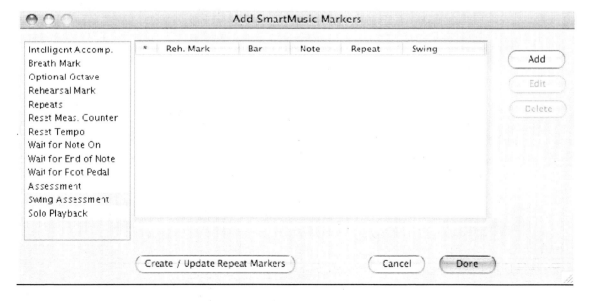

Apply Articulation...

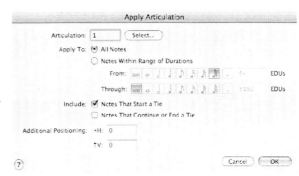

These utilities can also be used to apply articulations to a measure or group of measures. These function the same as when you click and drag the articulation tool on a measure without articulations.

- Choose which articulation you want to use: If you know the articulation number, enter it in the box, or click "Select…" and chose the one you want from the list.

- Select "All Notes" or the "Range of Durations" on which you want to place the articulation(s).

- Change the Tie Options if necessary.

- Additional Positioning can be used to place the articulations higher or lower and more toward the right or left of the note.

Exercise 8.9
Use Apply Articulation... to:

- Put "." staccato's on all the sixteenth notes.
- Put ">" accents only on the quarter notes (not the second tied note, though).
- Put "Tr" trills on all the half notes.

Check Notation Utilities:

The Check Notation submenu has several miscellaneous utilities that offer some unique functions:

Check Accidentals:

Hides any accidentals on notes tied over from the end of the previous measure, and adds accidentals, if necessary, on subsequent notes in the measure.

Check Elapsed Time:
Verifies the real-time length of the selected region of music or of the entire piece.

Check Ties:
Corrects all ties within the selected region <u>for playback only</u>.

Convert Mirrors:
Changes the selected mirror measures into normal non-mirrored measures.

Fill With Rests:
Checks a selected region of music for rhythmically incomplete measures and automatically fills them with the correct number of rests. Will not affect completely empty measures. This is a good utility to use before printing parts to make sure all the measures are complete.

Remove Manual Slur Adjustments:
Returns slurs to their default positions. Engraver slurs will reshape independently again.

Stem Direction:

Up/Down/Use Default Direction:
Forces all notes of a region to be stems up or down or, reverts them back to their default position.

Change Utilities:

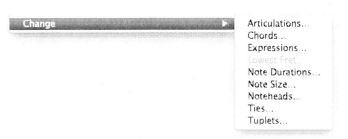

With the Selection Tool, click on any measure, and then Utilities → Change. The Change options let you change large sections of your music quickly instead of doing the change one measure at a time.

Articulations...	Allows you to replace one Articulation with another and/or reposition all articulations.

BEFORE: **AFTER**

Chords....	Allows you to change what parts of a chord are displayed and/or played. Also allows you to transpose chords and modify the positioning.

Expressions...	Allows you to replace one Expression with another and/or reposition all expressions.

BEFORE: **AFTER**

Lowest Fret...

When a region of a TAB staff is selected, recalculates the fret numbers to appear no lower than a specific fret.

Note Durations...	Allows you to change note values by either doubling or halving.

Original   **½ the value**   **2 times the value**

Note Size...	Changes the note size to a specific percentage.

BEFORE: **AFTER:**
at 100%   **at 50%**

Noteheads...

Replaces one notehead for another or changes all noteheads to normal or custom noteheads. This function is very useful for changing the noteheads of many measures at once.

BEFORE: **AFTER:**

Ties...

Allows you to change the tie directions and other options.

Tuplets...

Same as Tuplet tool, but affects only the measures you highlight. Does **NOT** create new Tuplets. This function is very useful if you want to change the appearance of many measures of tuplets without changing them one by one.

 # Staff Styles

---

Finale Terminology:

Staff Styles: Staff Styles are custom sets of staff attributes that can be applied to a measure region instead of the entire staff. Staff styles can be used to create transpositions, change the number of staff lines or the notation style for the selection region. They can also be used to hide layers or even the whole staff on a measure-by-measure basis. Staff Styles remain constant throughout the entire score. If you change a specific Staff Style, all regions that have that specific Staff Style applied to them will be affected.

To apply a Staff Style to a specific measure region:

- Select the Staff Tool.
- Click on any measure(s) (with or without music) to select the region where you wish to apply the style.
- Click Staff menu and then Apply Staff Style.
- Choose the Staff Style from the window.
- You can also apply more than one Staff Style to a measure and the effects will be added to each other (if possible).

Some commonly used Staff Styles are shown below:

Slash Notation
Hides the music in Layer 1, and replaces it with evenly spaced, stemless slashes that appear on each beat in the measure.

Rhythmic Notation
Converts every note or chord in Layer 1 to a slash or diamond-shaped notehead that is beamed and stemmed in the same rhythm.

Blank Notation: Layer 1
Hides the music in Layer 1.

Blank Notation: All Layers
Hides the music in all layers.

Normal Notation
Displays the music in all layers in standard music notation.

One-Bar Repeat(s)
Hides the music in all layers, and displays a one-measure repeat symbol in each measure.

Two-Bar Repeat(s)
Hides the music in all layers, and displays a two-measure repeat symbol for each pair of measures. You must have two measures selected with the Staff Tool for this option to work.

Removing Staff Styles

To remove a style, select the region with the Staff Tool, and select Staff → Clear Staff Styles.

Defining Your Own Staff Styles:

You can define your own custom Staff Style by selecting "Define Staff Styles..." and choosing the music items you want to show or hide.

Recognizing Staff Styles:

You can tell that a Staff Style is in effect by the blue bar above the music. Furthermore, if you have the "Show Staff Style Names" selected, it will also show you which one(s) are being used.

Example 8.10

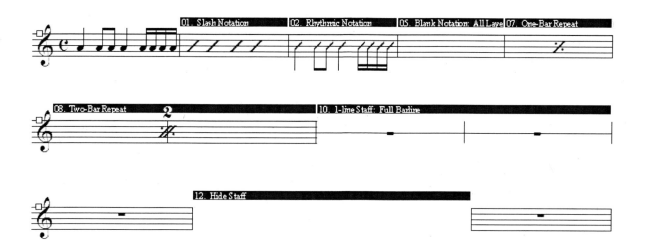

Putting it all together…

Reproduce the following example:

- Try to make the most of using the Selection Tool to copy repeated passages and to add octaves to existing notes.
- There are many Staff Styles being used below. Try to figure out which ones are used to accomplish the different notation styles.

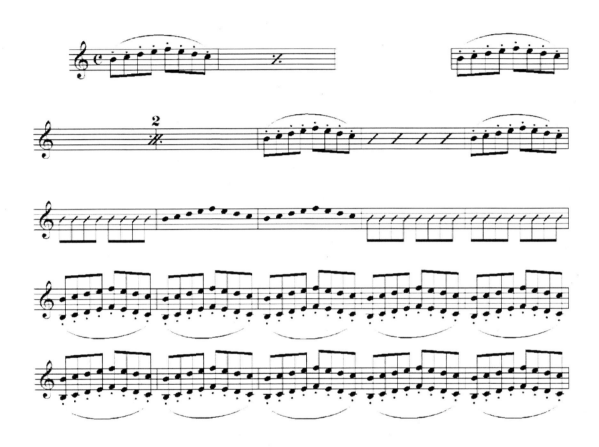

Chapter 9
More Advanced Tools

Tools covered in this chapter are listed below:

ADVANCED TOOLS:

Special Tools

Note Mover

Ossia Tool

Mirror Tool

SPECIAL TOOLS:

Note Position Tool		Notehead Position Tool
Note Shape Tool		Accidental Mover Tool
Stem Length Tool		Broken Beam Tool
Stem Direction Tool		Double Split Stem Tool
Reverse Stem Tool		Custom Stem Tool
Beam Angle Tool		Secondary Beam Break Tool
Beam Extension Tool		Secondary Beam Angle Tool
Tie Tool		Dot Tool
Beam Width Tool		Beam Stem Adjust Tool

Note Mover Tool

We have seen that you can use the Selection Tool to copy, paste, and further manipulate large amounts of data from several measures at one time. You can select either entire measures or portions of measures. The Note Mover Tool, on the other hand, moves and/or copies individual notes within a measure from one place to another. You can also use this tool to create Cross Staff notes often found in keyboard music, or to search for a note or group of notes and replace them with a different note or group of notes (Search and Replace).

The Note Mover Tool has several modes for copying and replacing:

Copy and Replace mode:
This mode copies the selected notes into the target measure by pasting them on the same beats as the source measure. All notes in the target measure (if there are any) are replaced regardless of how many or how few notes you copied from the source measure. Rests will be inserted to complete the measure where needed according to the current time signature. With the Note Mover tool selected, click on the measure from which you want to copy notes. Select the handles above the notes you want to copy. Then, drag one of the selected handles to the next measure to copy. **Remember! The notes you are copying will replace all the music in that measure.**

Before Using Copy and Replace:
Notes in the left measure have been selected and will be copied into the right measure.

After Using Copy and Replace:
The right measure now contains just the selected notes from the left measure and added rests to complete the measure.

Copy and Merge:

This mode copies the selected notes into the target measure by pasting them on the same beats as the source measure while existing music in the target measure remains. With the Note Mover tool selected, click on the measure from which you want to copy notes. Select the handles above the notes you would like to copy. Then drag one of the selected handles to the next measure to copy.

Before Using Copy and Merge:
Notes in the left measure have been selected and will be merged into the right measure.

After Using Copy and Merge:
The right measure now contains the selected notes from the left measure as well as the notes that were previously in the measure. Note how Finale has changed the durations of the notes in the right measure to accommodate the new notes.

Delete After Replace:

This mode functions the same as Copy and Replace, except that the original notes are deleted as shown here:

Before Using Delete After Replace:
Notes in the left measure have been selected and will be copied into the right measure and then deleted.

After Using Delete After Replace:
The right measure now contains just the selected notes from the left measure and added rests to complete the measure. The copied notes from the left measure have been deleted and changed to rests.

Delete After Merge:

This mode functions the same as Copy and Merge, except that the original notes are deleted as shown here:

Before Using Delete After Merge:
Notes in the left measure have been selected and will be merged into the right measure and then deleted.

After Using Deleted After Merge:
The right measure now contains the selected notes from the left measure as well as the notes that were previously in the measure. The notes copied from the left measure have been deleted and changed to rests.

Insert Before:

This mode pastes the selected notes at the beginning of the target measure regardless of their positions in the source measure. All previously existing notes are pushed to the right of the measure to accommodate the inserted notes. If the target measure is already full, extra notes will be deleted from the end of the target measure. This mode can also be used to copy notes from within the same measure.

Before Using Inserting Before:
Notes in the left measure have been selected and will be inserted before any notes at the beginning of the right measure.

After Using Insert Before:
The right measure now begins with the three notes that were selected from the left measure. The notes that already existed in the right measure have moved over to make room for the new notes. Any extra notes that would give the measure too many beats (according to the time signature) have been deleted.

Append After:

This mode pastes the selected notes at the end of the target measure. **Important! If the target measure is already full, this command will have no effect and the target measure will not be changed.** Therefore, there must be enough room in the target measure to accommodate the notes that you are appending.

Before Using Append After:
Notes in the left measure have been selected and will be appended after the notes in the right measure.

After Using Append After:
The right measure now contains the notes that were previously in the measure as well as the three selected notes appended at the end.

Cross Staff:

The Note Mover tool also allows you to move the note head to a staff above or below where it was originally created. **Important! The notes always exist in the staff where they were originally created. Therefore, you can only edit them in the staff where they were first created and not the staff in which they are currently showing.**

To make a Cross Staff note:

- With the Note Mover tool selected, select Cross Staff from the Note Mover Menu.
- Click on the measure with the note(s) you want to move to another staff.
- Click on the handle above the note(s) that you want to move.
- Finish creating the Cross Staff by dragging one of the highlighted handles to the staff above or the staff below.

This becomes............ this after using Cross Staff.

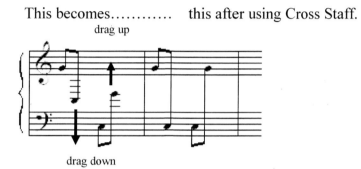

Exercise 9.1: Make a Cross Staff measure with the original notes in the upper staff and one with the original notes in the lower staff similar to this:

Hints: There are no default whole rests in some of these measures even though they have no notes in them. How can you hide the whole rests where needed?

Search and Replace

In addition to the copy, merge, insert and append modes, the Note Mover also has a search and replace mode. (In reality, it is more like a search and modify mode). With it, you can search for a single note or a group of notes. You can also limit your search to find the notes in the same octave as the originals or in any octave. And, you can limit the search to match durations with the original notes. For example, if the search note is a quarter note, then all matches must also be quarter notes.

<u>Using the Note Mover to find a note or group of notes:</u>
1. Select the Note Mover Tool.
2. Click on the measure that contains the note or notes you wish to find.
3. Select the note or pattern of notes you wish to find by clicking the handles above the notes.

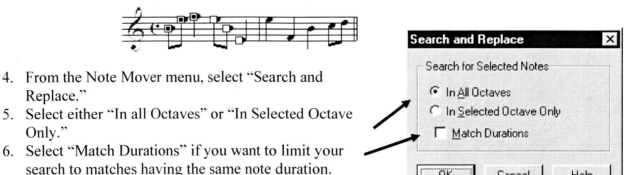

4. From the Note Mover menu, select "Search and Replace."
5. Select either "In all Octaves" or "In Selected Octave Only."
6. Select "Match Durations" if you want to limit your search to matches having the same note duration.
7. Click OK.
8. Click OK again skipping over the Slot Alteration dialog box. (We'll get to that soon.)
9. A new menu will appear called "Search." Select the "Find" option on this new menu.

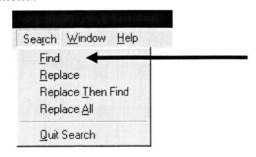

This will search through your entire document and stop at the next instance matching the search pattern you specified.

In addition to searching for notes, you can also perform a few simple alterations on the notes that you find.

Finale Terminology:

<u>Slot</u>: Each note in your search pattern is referred to as a slot. The first note in your pattern fills slot 1. The second note in your pattern fills slot 2 and so on.

You can perform one of two alterations on each slot in your search group or you can choose perform no alteration slot which is the default action. Each slot can either be transposed (chromatically or diatonically), or changed to its enharmonic equivalent. Therefore, if you wanted to replace all the A's in your piece to B's, you could choose to diatonically transpose them up a second. If you wanted all of your C's to become C-sharp's, chromatically transpose them up an augmented unison. Similarly, you can change all your C-sharp's to D-flat's by doing an enharmonic alteration on that slot. You can also quickly specify the same alteration for all slots by clicking the "Set All" button.

<u>Using the Note Mover to find and replace a note or group of notes:</u>

- Follow the first seven steps above to set up a search pattern.
- When you get to the Slot Alteration box, choose either Transpose or Enharmonic to alter that specific slot.
- If you do not want to alter the current Slot, leave the setting on "No Transposition."
- Use the "Prev" and "Next" buttons to cycle through the Slots in your search group and make any other alterations you wish. If you have only one note in your search pattern, you will only see one Slot and these buttons will be grayed out.
- Click OK.
- A new menu will appear called "Search." Select the option on this new menu to choose what you would like to do.

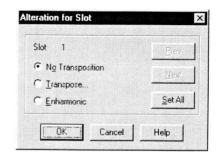

"Replace" will replace the currently selected notes.

"Replace Then Find" will replace the currently selected notes and then search for the next occurrence.

"Replace All" scours your entire piece replacing all matches it finds.

Note: After performing a "Replace All," your music will be scrolled to the end of the piece. This is because Finale is searching through your entire piece looking for matches.

Exercise 9.2:

Using the Note Mover Tool:

- First, change all of the E-flats to D-sharps with Search and Replace.

- Transpose all the A's down an octave and all the E's up an octave.

Ossia Tool

An Ossia is an alternative version of a musical passage or, in some instances, a simplified or ornamented version of the same music. The Ossia Tool in Finale allows you to create just such a measure. These measures are called "floating measures" because they are not part of any system and can be placed anywhere on the page. However, they are always based on existing music so the music that creates them must already exist somewhere in the score. Most of the time, the source music for the Ossia is hidden using a hidden staff or creative page layouts. You can only create one Ossia Measure at a time. With careful positioning, you can place several Ossia Measures back to back to make them appear like several continuous measures or another line of music. If you need to make a long string of Ossia Measures, it might be a better idea to consider using an additional staff instead.

There are a few things to keep in mind when planning Ossia Measures:
- Ossia Measures always need a real (source) measure.
- Ossia Measures do not produce any playback.
- Ossia Measures can be assigned to either a measure or a page.
- Measure Assigned Ossias are always the same width as their source measure.
- Page Assigned Ossias can vary in width and often need to be resized to properly fit above existing music.
- Smart Shapes such as slurs **do not** appear in Ossias.

Exercise 9.3 Scroll View Example:

OSSIA MEASURE →

To make the Ossia Measure:
- **In Scroll View,** select the Ossia Tool.
- Click the measure where you want to attach the Ossia Measure.
- Specificy the Source Staff and Source Measure.
- Make any display changes for the Ossia Measure.
- Click "OK" twice.
- Position the Ossia Measure where you want it.
- Hide the source: With the Staff Tool, double click
  the source staff. Then select "Hide Staff."

SOURCE
MEASURE →

Ossia Measures are usually printed at a reduced size unlike the surrounding music. You can accomplish this by changing the "Scale To" setting in the Display Settings section of the Ossia Measure Designer window. You can also change the appearance of several other aspects of the Ossia Measure such as the Bracket, Key Signature, Time Signature, Clef, and Right Barline. Additionally, you can hide or show other items including Endings and Text Repeats, Left Barline, Time Signature, Key Signature, Clefs, Expressions, and Staff.

PAGE VIEW EXAMPLE:

If you are working in Page View, Ossia Measures will be assigned to pages instead of measures by default. They function the same as when assigned to measures, except their width must be set. You can specify the Ossia Measure width when you are creating it, or you can change the width of an existing page assigned Ossia Measure by shift-double clicking on the handle of the Ossia Measure.

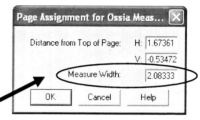

Hint: Instead of using a trial and error approach to find the proper measure width for the Ossia, use the Measure Tool and double click on the measure you are placing over the Ossia. The width displayed in the window will be the width of the measure. Set your Ossia Measure to this width for a perfect fit.

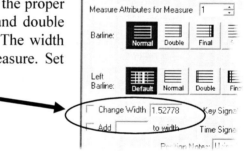

Exercise 9.4 Page View Example:

Produce the following Ossia in Page View. Remember to hide the source measure. Find the proper Ossia Measure width by using the Measure Tool. Make the Ossia Measure the proper width and line it up properly above the real notes.

It is possible to create a whole line of music using back to back Ossia Measures if you are very careful in how you place them. Remember, some will need a left barline and some will need a right barline only. You will most likely have to hide the time signature, key signature, and clef in all but the first Ossia Measure. If you need more than just a few back-to-back Ossia Measures, using another staff might be a better idea. Use Staff Optimization to hide the staff when it's not being used.

Exercise 9.5 Creating Back to Back Ossia Measures

Carefully placed Ossia Measures can create a floating line of music anywhere in your score.

Special Tools

One of Finale's greatest strengths lies in its set of Special Tools. With these tools, you can do such things as make small adjustments to the heads or stems of individual notes, change the angle of a beam, or beam notes over the barline. These tools are indispensable when working with contemporary music.

Below is the list of Special Tools. Some are easy to figure out. Others are more elusive and sometimes downright strange. We will look at each Special Tool in detail so you can get an idea of what it can do for you.

Note Position Tool		**Notehead Position Tool**
Note Shape Tool		**Accidental Mover Tool**
Stem Length Tool		**Broken Beam Tool**
Stem Direction Tool		**Double Split Stem Tool**
Reverse Stem Tool		**Custom Stem Tool**
Beam Angle Tool		**Secondary Beam Break Tool**
Beam Extension Tool		**Secondary Beam Angle Tool**
Tie Tool		**Dot Tool**
Beam Width Tool		**Beam Stem Adjust Tool**

The Special Tools can be found either by clicking on the "hammer, wrench, and screwdriver" icon on the main tool palette, or in newer versions of Finale, they can be found on the Advanced Tool Palette found under the Tools menu.

All Special Tools work the same way:
- Select the Special Tool you want to use.
- Click on the measure that contains the notes you want to target.
- Select the notes you want to modify by clicking on the handles that appear above the notes.
- To delete/remove any changes you made, either unselect the handles you selected or press "Delete" on your keyboard when the handles are selected.

Note Position Tool

- Allows you to move any note left or right.
- Use the handles to drag notes left or right.
- Moves the entire note (head and stem) or the entire chord.
- Works the same as dragging a note in Speedy Entry.
- Only moves notes in one measure; other notes on the same beat or part of a beat in measures above or below the music do not move. If you want to move all notes on a specific part of a beat, use the Note Positioning Chart with the Measure Tool.
- Shift-click to select more than one note to move at a time.
- Restore the note's default position by hitting Delete when it is selected.

 Notehead Position Tool

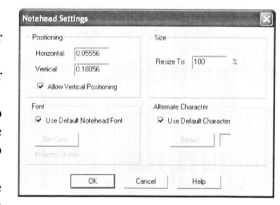

- Allows you to move only the notehead left or right of any note or chord.
- Use the handles to drag the notehead left or right.
- Double-click on the handle above the note to specify exact numerical values, resize the notehead, allow vertical positioning, and to change the notehead's font or shape.
- Use this tool to switch noteheads from one side of a chord to the other or to fine tune tone cluster chords.
- Hit Delete on any selected handle to restore the notehead to its default position.

Note Shape Tool

- Allows you to change the head of any note to any shape or symbol.
- Double-click on the handle by the notehead and select the symbol you wish to use.
- You can also click more than one handle or highlight several handles to change more than one notehead at a time.
- Use this tool to make measured tremolos (as shown below).
- To remove noteheads altogether, pick the space (character 32) for the notehead shape.
- If you need to change the noteheads of several measures, use the Utilities menu and the Change Notehead command.
- Hit Delete on any selected handle to change it back to the default notehead.

 Accidental Mover Tool

- Allows you to move accidentals left or right.
- Drag the handle next to the accidental to the left or right to move it.
- Double-click on the handle to specify exact numerical values, resize the accidental, allow vertical positioning, and to change the font and accidental character (similar to the Note Position Tool, see above).
- This tool is useful for adjusting accidentals in chords or where several accidentals appear close together. Position them so that they are easier to read.
- Hit Delete on any selected handle to change it back to its default position.

Stem Length Tool

- Lengthens or shortens the stem of a single (unbeamed) note.
- Drag the handle up or down to lengthen or shorten a stem.
- Hit Delete on any handle to remove the stem length modification.
- Can also be used to remove a stem completely by shortening the stem all the way back to the notehead.

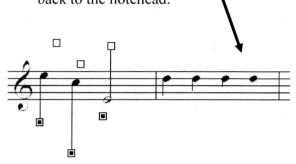

 Broken Beam Tool

- Flips a beam stub (sixteenth note or smaller) to the other side of the stem.
- Useful in triple meters (3/8, 6/8, 9/8, etc.)
- Hit Delete to restore the stub back to its default position.

 Stem Direction Tool

- "Freezes" the direction of a stem (that's why it looks like a snowflake).
- Similar to using "L" key in Speedy Entry.
- Click the upper handle to freeze the stem up or lower handle to freeze it.
- Unselecting the handle will restore the default stem direction for the note.

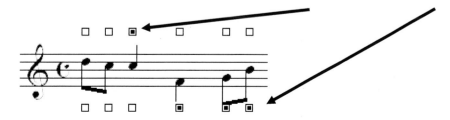

Double/Split Stem Tool

- Adds a second stem in the opposite direction to a note or chord.
- Can split the stem from the notehead if there are two or more notes.
- Click either outer handle to draw a second stem.
- To separate notes: First click on the **lower handle** to create a second stem. Then click the notehead handles on the notes you want to split to the upper stem (see first and third beats below).
- Unselecting the handles will remove the added double stem(s).

BEFORE: **AFTER:**

Split Stem------------Not Split--Split Stem

 Reverse Stem Tool

- Flips the stem from one side of the note to the other.
- Click a handle either above or below the note to move the stem to the other side of the notehead.
- Useful when working with Cross Staff Notes. **Remember: If no notes are in the measure where the Cross Staff notes are moving, you must hide the default whole rest**. One way would be to put a rest or note in that measure and hide it with the "O" key in Speedy Entry.
- Use the Reverse Stem Tool in conjunction with the Beam Angle Tool to position the beam properly between the upper and lower notes (see below).
- Reverse Stemming can be turned on or off entirely by clicking "Display Reverse Stemming" in the Document Options under the Document Settings menu.
- To remove Reverse Stemming, unselect the handles you used to turn it on.

Use with the Note Mover's Cross Staff function to create keyboard music like this:

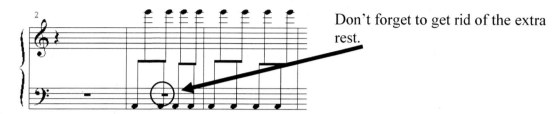

Don't forget to get rid of the extra rest.

 Custom Stem Tool

- Creates a custom stem for a note.
- Select one or more handles, then double-click a handle to display the Shape Selection dialog box where you can choose or create a replacement stem shape.
- Once a Custom Stem is created, you can move it by dragging the handle so that the stem is properly positioned.
- You can also use this tool to hide the stem of a note—just create a blank shape. Break the beam if you want to show no beam when using blank stems.
- To remove the custom stem, select it and then hit delete.

Examples of custom stems and blank stems:

Beam Angle Tool

- The Beam Angle Tool allows you to change the height of beams as well as their angle.
- Drag the left handle up or down to change the beam height and in turn the stem length under the beam. The right handle will also move so that the beam angle does not change.
- Drag the right handle up or down to change the beam angle.

Changing beam height:

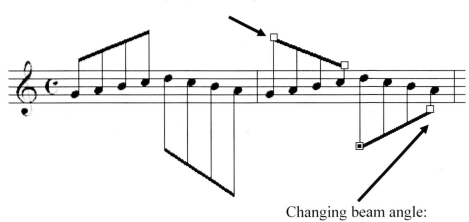

Changing beam angle:

- The Beam Angle Tool is also used when doing Cross Staff notes to properly position the beam.
- The notes in the top staff of the first measure below have had their stems reversed with the Reverse Stem Tool, but they look unprofessional. The beams need to be moved down as shown in the second measure using the Beam Angle Tool.

Before: **After:**

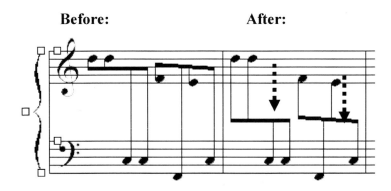

Secondary Beam Break Tool

- The Secondary Beam Break Tool is used to break sixteenth and smaller note beams. (You have already learned that you can use the "/" key in Speedy Entry to break the primary eighth note beam and all other attached beams.)
- Double-click a handle to display the Secondary Beam Break Selection dialog box where you can break sixteenth notes or smaller beams.
- To turn off secondary beam breaks, unclick the handles you selected.

Before: After:

- When specifying the break level, you have the option to break through all beams as shown above or to break only a certain beam as shown below:

Break Level:
- No Break
- Break ONLY 16th
- Break ONLY 32nd
- Break ONLY 64th
- Break THROUGH 16th
- Break THROUGH 32nd
- Break THROUGH 64th
- No Break

 Beam Extension Tool

- The Beam Extension tool allows you to extend a beam past its last note.
- The eighth note beam is extended by default unless you double-click a handle and select which beam(s) to extend.
- Use this tool with the Beam Angle Tool (see above) to beam across barlines as shown below.
- Hit Delete to remove any Beam Extensions you have created.

Extending various beams

Beaming across the barline: First extend the beam(s), then use the Beam Angle tool to match the heights and angles of the beams.

Secondary Beam Angle Tool

- The Secondary Beam Angle Tool works much the same as the Beam Angle Tool, EXCEPT it moves all the beams other than the eighth note beams.
- Drag the <u>left handle</u> to change the beam height.
- Drag the <u>right handle</u> to change the beam angle.
- Hitting Delete restores the beam height and angle back to their default positions.
- Using a combination of adjustments to the left and right handles, you can create the feathered beams show below:

 Tie Tool

- The Tie Tool allows you to manipulate the starting and ending points of a tie as well as the height of the tie's arc.
- You can double-click either the left or right tie handles to enter exact numerical values and to specify other options (see below).
- You can use this tool to flip a tie over or under notes. Double-click the left or right tie handle and specify tie direction. Or, use CTRL-F on PC or COMMAND-F on Mac to flip the tie.
- If you double click on the arc-adjusting (middle) handle, a second handle will appear. Each handle will then control half the tie's arc for further adjustments.

Drag the left or right handles to adjust the start or end of the tie.
Drag the middle handle to change the arc.
Flip ties for better readability of chords.

- You can set precise values for the starting and ending points of the tie and the horizontal and vertical placement by using the Tie Alterations box.
- You can specify if Finale breaks ties across Time and Key Signatures and uses Outer Placement settings as defined in Tie Options under Document Settings.
- The Avoid Staff Lines button ensures that ties do not fall right on staff lines for better readability.

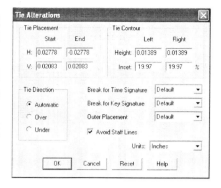

 Dot Tool

- The Dot Tool allows you to precisely position one or more augmentation dots.
- On a single dot, drag the handle to position the dot.
- On two or more dots, the left handle moves the position of all the dots; the right handle increases or decreases the spacing between the dots.
- Double-click a handle to make exact numerical adjustments to the augmentation dots.
- Hit Delete (or Reset from the Dots Offset Dialog Box) to reset the dot(s) back to the original position(s).

Drag the left (or only) handle to move the first dot away from the note.

Drag the right handle to change the distance between the dots if there is more than one.

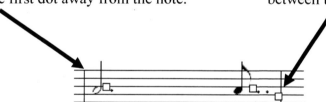

Beam Width Tool

- The Beam Width Tool changes the width or thickness of all the beams in a group of notes.
- Drag the handles to increase or decrease the width of the beams.
- If you make the beams thin enough, they will disappear altogether (see the second beat of the right measure below).
- If the beams become so thick that you can no longer see the separation between the eighth and sixteenth note beams, use the Secondary Beam Angle Tool (see previous page) to make room between them (see the third beat of the right measure below).
- You can reset the beams to their default width, by hitting Delete when one of the handles is selected.

Drag the handles to change the width of the beam in a group of notes.

Before: After:

Beams removed.

 Beam Stem Adjust Tool

- This tool changes the length and position of a stem under a beam. (For single notes, use the Stem Length Tool).
- Drag the handle up or down to change the length of a stem under a beam.
- You can move the stem left or right by dragging the handle.
- You can select all the handles of a group of notes to move them as a unit.
- To remove any adjustments, hit Delete on a selected handle.

Before: After:

 # Mirror Tool

---

Finale Terminology:

Mirror: A Mirror is an intelligent copy of music. It is intelligent in that when the original changes, the mirror copy also changes. Like reflected images in a real mirror, mirror copies cannot be edited. The original must be edited instead. Mirrors can get very complex by omitting notes from the original, using notes from more than one measure, and even transposing notes from the original.

How to create a simple mirror copy:

- Select the Mirror Tool.
- Select "Dragging Mirrors Measures" from the Mirror menu.
- Select Drag the measure with the music one measure to the right.
- Click "OK" to NOT make any changes to the music (we'll learn more about the mirror's other options later in this chapter).
- Change any of the notes in the first (original) measure and watch what happens to the mirrored (copy) measure.

Exercise 9.6

Original: **Mirror Copy**

Notice how the mirror copy changes when the original changes.

Changed Original: **Mirror Copy**

The Mirror Tool also has an additional function other than creating mirrored measures. It can create a Placeholder that is used to create pickup measures anywhere in your score.

How does the Mirror Tool know if you want to create a Placeholder or a Mirror? If the measure you double-click on already contains notes, you will create a Placeholder. If the measure is empty or contains a mirror, you will begin to create a Mirror in that measure.

Finale Terminology:

Placeholder: A *Placeholder* is Finale's way of keeping track of the beat(s) needed to make a complete measure when you have pickup notes. All notes after a Placeholder are pushed to the right of the measure becoming pickup notes. Note: if the pickup measure is the first measure of the piece, use "Pickup Measure…" under the Document menu instead. The Placeholder icon looks like a dinner place setting to remind you that it's holding the place of other notes.

Creating Pickup Measures with the Mirror Tool:

- With the Mirror Tool selected, click on the measure that contains the pickup notes. **Note: the pickup notes must already be in the measure or Finale will think you want to create a Mirror.**
- Calculate the number of beats you need to put before the pick-up notes in order to make a full measure. This is called the "Placeholder."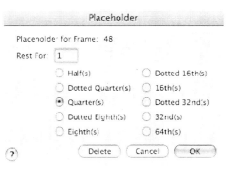
- Click the note value that equals the amount you calculated in step two. For 3 beats, for example, you could either enter 3 quarter notes or 2 dotted quarters or even 6 eighths.
- Click "OK."
- Specify if the Placeholder will apply to only this staff or all staves.
- Click "OK."

WITHOUT Pickup Place holder:

WITH Pickup Place holder:

When you create the Placeholder, you can place it either on all staves or on a single staff. Therefore, you could have a different duration Placeholder on each staff if needed. If you use the "Pickup Measure…" option under the Document menu, only the first measure will have the pickup and all staves will have the same length pickup.

Finale Terminology:

Custom Mirror: A *Custom Mirror* is copy of a single measure that is linked to that measure in such a way that when the source measure changes, the Mirror copy changes as well. Just like trick mirrors, what you see in the mirror may or may not be an exact copy of the original. Custom Mirror copies can be selective, taking only parts of the original and leaving others out. They also can vary from the original by transposing the original notes, hiding certain elements, rebeaming, etc.

Custom Mirrors:

You can use the Mirror Attributes window to change the mirrored copy. You might for example transpose the mirror or hide certain musical elements.

In the example below, the measure on the left is the source measure. The measure on the right is a mirror with these Mirror Attributes:

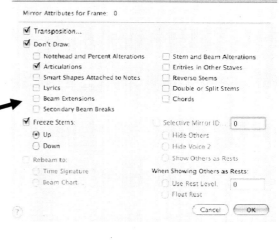

Source Measure   Custom Mirror

Creating Composite Mirrors:

We learned earlier that you use the Mirror Tool if you want to make a Mirror copy that is one complete measure. Finale also lets you make Mirrors that are much more elaborate by taking notes from many different measures using the Mirror Tool.

Finale Terminology:

Composite Mirror: This is a special kind of Mirror comprised of one or more notes from any measure in the score. For example, it can contain two notes from beat four of measure two in staff one, and four notes from measure fifty-two in staff eight.

Tilting Mirror: While it sounds like yet another kind of Mirror, a Tilting Mirror is just the name of the window used to create Composite Mirrors. You navigate this window around your score using the up, down, left, and right arrows jumping from measure to measure, staff to staff, and layer to layer. You then select the notes you wish to add to your composite Mirror by enclosing them in the left and right vertical bars and clicking OK, or Next (if you want to add other notes).

How to create a Composite Mirror:

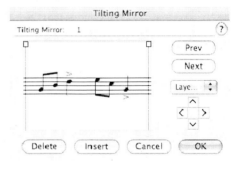

- Double-click a blank measure with the Mirror Tool. This will bring up the Tilting Mirror window. (Remember if you click a measure containing notes, Finale will start to make a Placeholder).
- When you first start using the Tilting Mirror window, it is initially blank because you are starting in the measure where you are creating the Mirror which is also blank.
- Use the left, right, up, and down arrows in the window to move throughout your score to select the note(s) you want to be in your Mirror. You can also change the layer by using the dropdown menu.
- Use the bars on the left and right of the Tilting Mirror window to frame the notes you want to choose by dragging them left and right to enclose the notes.
- To add more notes to your Mirror from the current measure or another measure, click the "Next" button.
- To add notes before a previous set of notes, click "Insert."
- You can cycle through the groups of notes you have already created with the "Prev" and "Next" buttons. If you find one you don't want, click the "Delete" button to get rid of it.
- When you are completely finished, click "OK."
- You can then specify any other options for the Mirror copy such as transposition, stem freezing, etc.
- Click "OK" to finish creating the Mirror.

You can tell that a measure contains a Mirror copy because of the Mirror icon that appears when the Mirror Tool is selected. You **will not** be able to edit any of the notes or other symbols in the Mirror copy with any of the note edit tools. Like looking into a real mirror, the image is a reflection and not a real object. The same is true with Mirrors in Finale. There are not real notes in mirrored measures—just reflections of other measures. (You can turn them into real notes, however. See Chapter 8 on converting Mirrors).

The following composite Mirror was made up of the third through sixth notes in the second measure (the notes in the square) and the first three notes in the first measure (the notes in the circle). The resulting composite Mirror (the third measure) contains all the included notes.

Exercise 9.7

Another benefit to composite Mirrors is that the mirrored notes do not have to be used exactly as they are. There are several other options such as transposition, rebeaming, hiding various notational elements, and Selective Mirror ID's that you can use to change and format the mirrored notes.

<u>Other Options:</u>

Transposition

- Determines whether to transpose the entire Mirror relative to the original material either chromatically or diatonically up or down.

Don't Draw:

- <u>Notehead or Percent Alterations</u>- Won't draw any changes you made to notehead shapes with the Note Shape Tool or notehead percent changes with the Resize Tool.
- <u>Articulations and Staff Expressions</u>- Won't draw articulations or any staff expressions already attached to notes.
- <u>Slurs Attached to Notes</u>- Won't draw any slurs you created by double-clicking on a note and dragging the slur to another note.
- <u>Lyrics</u>- Won't draw any text you entered with the Lyric Tool.
- <u>Beam Extensions</u>- Won't draw any beams you extended with the Beam Extension Tool (see above).

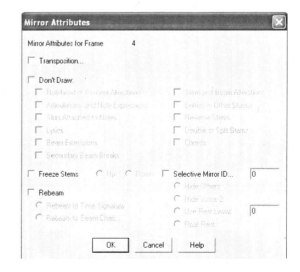

- Secondary Beam Breaks- Won't draw any sixteenth or smaller beams you broke with the Secondary Beam Break Tool (see above).
- Stem and Beam Alterations- Won't draw any changes to the note stem or beam made with any of the Special Tools.
- Entries in Other Staves- Won't draw any Cross Staff notes. Notes will appear as they were originally entered but without being Cross Staffed.
- Reverse Stems- Won't draw any notes you modified with the Reverse Stem Tool (see above).
- Double or Split Stems- Won't draw any notes you modified with the Double/Split Stem Tool on (see above).
- Chords- Won't draw any chord symbols or fretboards.

Freeze Stems: Up, Down
- Flips all stems in the Mirror up or all down.

Rebeam
- Rebeams the notes in the Mirror. You can either rebeam all the notes in the Mirror according to the current Time Signature or by using a custom Beaming Chart. **Note: When you select notes from a measure using the Tilting Mirror window, they retain the beaming they had in their original form. Therefore, they may not be beamed properly in the Mirror unless you select Rebeam from the Mirror Attributes window.**
- You can create a custom beaming pattern by selecting "Rebeam to Beam Chart." Click the handle above the note where you want to break a beam, and start a new group of beamed notes. Notes that are not selected will be beamed together with the previous selected note. **Note: the screen does not update after you click a handle to show what the new beaming will look like.** This only happens after you save the Mirror.

Mirror using Beam to Time Signature:

Mirror using Beaming Chart (see right):

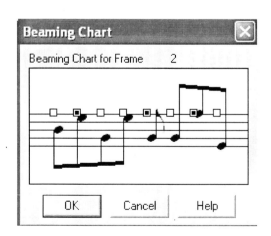

One final option you have when using Mirrors is defining a Selective Mirror ID.

Finale Terminology:

Selective Mirror: Another option of a Mirror in which you can select the notes of the Mirror you would like to display (such as the top notes of a chordal passage). Other notes not displayed are changed to rests, or are not shown at all, depending on the options you choose. You can define several Selective Mirror ID's for each Mirror. You specify which one you would like to use in the Mirror Attributes window by selecting its ID number.

To Use:

- Create your Mirror as you normally would (see previous page).
- In the Mirror Attributes window, click Selective Mirror ID.
- From the Selective Mirror window (see right), click the notes you want to show. Don't click the notes you want to hide. When dealing with chords, you can drag a selection around the entire chord or select only the notes of the chord you want to be displayed.

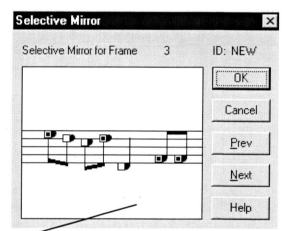

- If you want to create additional Selective Mirrors, click Next and proceed again to step three.
- Click OK to finish creating a Selective Mirror.

When dealing with Selective Mirrors, you have a few more options to consider when choosing how to display the notes:

Hide Others

- Shows blank notes/beats instead of rests for the notes/beats you omitted from the Selective Mirror.

Hide Voice 2

- Hides notes in Voice 2 in the Selective Mirror instead of displaying them as rests.

Use Rest Level

- Specifies where rests should appear in this Mirror. The number entered here specifies how high the rests will be placed as counted from the root scale tone and measured in lines and spaces. The larger the number, the higher the rests will be displayed.

Float Rest

- Places rests in the usual position.

Editing existing Mirrors:

If you need to edit a Mirror you have previously created, select the Mirror Tool and click on the measure with the Mirror icon. This will take you back to the Tilting Mirror window where you can add, delete, or make changes to the notes that comprise the Composite Mirror.

If you need to edit any details in the Mirror Attributes window, **shift-click** on the measure with the Mirror icon. This will take you directly to the Mirror Attributes window.

Putting It All Together…

Using what your learned in this chapter, reproduce the follow musical example.

Hints:

- Many of the Special Tools are needed to complete this exercise.
- The Note Mover and Ossia Tools are also needed.
- Create three staves in your score to reproduce the music. Optimize the systems to remove the bass clef staff from all but the second line where it is needed. The source staff for the Ossia Measure must also be removed or otherwise hidden.

Tools covered in this chapter are listed below:

Repeat Tool

Tempo Tool

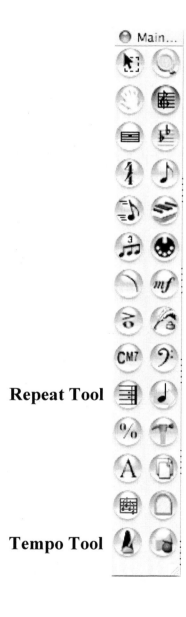

Instant Playback

The easiest way to instantly play a section of your music is to hold down the SPACE BAR and click the measure where you want playback to start.

Playback Controls

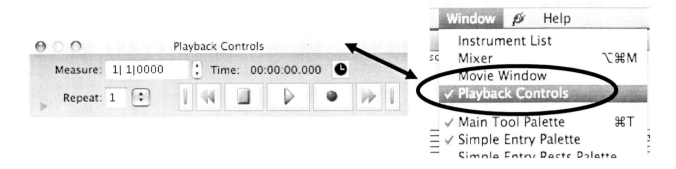

Use these controls to control playback by clicking tape deck-like buttons.

|	Rewinds to the beginning or the end.
<<	Rewinds. Click and hold to rewind incrementally.
>>	Fast Forward. Click and hold to advance incrementally.
Stop	Stops playback.
Play	Starts playback or, if playback is already started, pauses playback. You can also press the Space bar to Play/Pause.
Record	Starts recording at the specified measure using the HyperScribe Tool.
Measure #	Indicates the current measure (using Measure | Beat | Tick) during playback or sets the starting measure for playback or HyperScribe recording.
Time:	Shows the current time (in second and milliseconds if the clock is showing or seconds and frames if the film is showing).
Repeat:	Specifies the time through (first time, second time, etc) if repeats are used in your piece.

Other Options:

Expand the basic playback windows, click the Little Speaker or Small Triangle

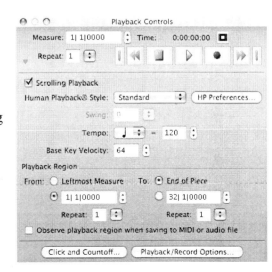

Play Mode:

- "Non-Scrolling"- music doesn't scroll while being played.

- "Scrolling" –scrolls back while playing.

Human Playback® Style:

These settings allow you to customize performance techniques, such as pizzicato or flutter tongue. They also provide a way to take advantage of a given sound library and allow you to specify settings for an individual playback device. Using these settings, Human Playback is capable of detailed changes to the playback and can take full advantage of any combination of sound devices.

Tempo:

Choose the note value from the drop-down list, enter a tempo in the text box, or click the up and down arrows to change the current tempo.

Base Key Velocity:

Determines the overall dynamic level. Enter a key velocity in the text box or click the up and down arrows to change the current velocity from 0 – 127.

Swing:

Enter the amount of swing you want in the box. A value of 200 works well. Hint: The higher the number, the later the second note in a swing pair and the heavier the swing. Duration determines the durational value of the notes to which you are applying swing. 512 = one eighth note; 1024 = one quarter note. If you are unsure, click on Swing Values to see a palette of possible durations.

Playback Region:

Allows you to specify the beginning and ending measures for playback or to begin at the right most measure and/or end at the end of the piece.

Click and Countoff:

Opens the Click and Countoff dialog box where you can choose various clicks for playback, recording, or both.

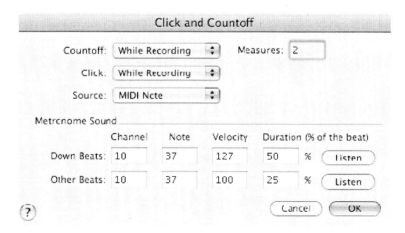

Playback/Record Options:

Opens the Playback Options dialog box where you can configure the playback of Recorded Key Velocities, Note Durations, Continuous Data, and Tempo Changes. You can also set the playback to ignore repeats (play right through them without observing the repeats) and reset repeats (treat them as the first time they are encountered).

Exercise 10.1

Open your own Finale file to become familiar with the playback controls. Try scrolling and non-scrolling playback. Try starting the piece at the beginning, or set it to play at the left bar. Also, change the tempo and base key velocity to see what happens.

 # Tempo Changes

When using playback to hear your score, you may need to change the tempo in the middle of the piece. You can do this in several ways. These methods also work to set the tempo at the beginning of the piece.

Expression Method:

Using an Expression, you can set or change the tempo of your score anytime.

- Create or edit an existing Expression.
- Click "Playback" tab in the Expression Designer window.
- Set Type to Tempo.
- Choose a note value (quarter note, eighth note).
- Set to Value = 120.

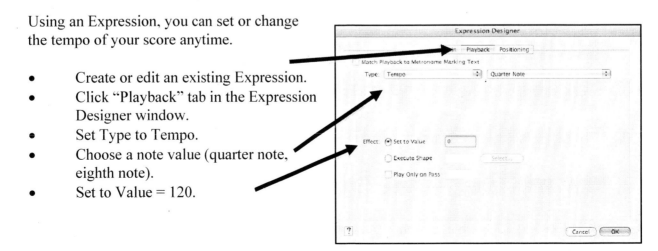

Gradually Changing the Tempo: Human Playback Method

If your score is configured to use Human Playback® (see earlier information this chapter), many tempo changes will already function automatically. Below are all the tempo change markings which Finale understands and will automatically perform. All you need to do to use one of them is to make an Expression using any of the word(s) below:

acc, accel, accelerando, accelerato, affretando, incalzando, ristringendo, stringendo, string, stretto, en pressant, pressez, en accélérant, faster, beschleunigend, eilend, drängend, belebend, rall, rallentando, calando, rit, ri, ritar, riten, ritenuto, ritenente, ritardando, slargando, morendo, ritardo, allargando, allarg, retenu, rallentir, en retenant, en cédant, cédez, zurückhaltend, breiterwerdend, breiter, a tempo, tempo, on time, au mouvement, zeitmass, zeitmaß

These can also be further modified with the following directions:

poco a poco, peu à peu, nach und nach, little by little, sempre, toujours, always, immer, molto, moltissimo, moltiss, très, beaucoup, much, un poco, poco, pochissimo, poch, un peu, légèrement, etwas, a little

Execute Shape Method

You can have Finale speed up or slow down the music by selecting "Execute Shape" instead of "Set to Value." "Accel." and "Rit." are already setup for you. You can use any shape to affect the tempo. If the shape goes higher than its starting point, the tempo will increase. If the shape goes lower, the tempo will decrease. See the Executable Shape Designer on the following page for fine-tuning the way Finale uses the shape data.

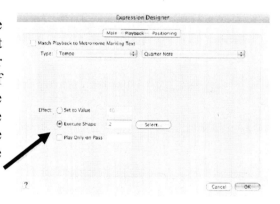

accel.   *rit.*   *Variable*

Using the Executable Shape Designer:

When you choose to execute a shape to control the tempo or some other aspect of the music, you need to tell Finale how the change in the shape relates to the change in the parameter. You may do this by setting the variables in the Executable Shape Designer to control the Time and Level Scale and sample rate. These variables are discussed in depth below:

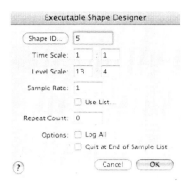

Shape ID- The shape number you are going to use to control Finale. Click the Shape ID button and then choose a shape.

Time Scale- Refers to how often Finale looks at the shape measure in eighth notes. By default, this is once every eighth note, but you can change that interval here as shown below:

Time Scale Ratio	Frequency
1:1	Each eighth note
1:2	Each sixteenth note
2:1	Each quarter note
4:1	Each half note

Level Scale- The ratio of how much the affected parameter is changed by the shape. For example, a 1:1 ratio will change tempo (in beats per minute) one beat per minute for each one increase or decrease of the shape. Some examples using tempo are shown below:

Level Scale Ratio	Change in Tempo
1:1	1 BPM per change in shape
1:2	1 BPM per 2 changes in shape
2:1	2 BPM's per change in shape
10:1	10 BPM's per change in shape

Sample Rate- Allows you to further fine tune how often the parameter is changed by using every other sample change or every third sample change or every Nth sample change. The value you enter here will determine how many shape samples must change before the parameter is affected.

Use List- Allows you to enter a list of up to six values used to vary the Sample Rate. For example "1, 1, 3, 7" would force Finale to wait to change the parameter for 1 sample, then 1 sample, then 3 samples and then 7 samples. This list is repeated as many times as needed to cover all data in the shape.

Repeat Count- How many times you want to play shape.

Log All- Forces Finale to change the parameter, even when no change in the shape occurs (such as a flat line).

Quit at End of Sample List- Forces Finale to end changing the parameter when the Sample List (see above) ends. Therefore, when this option is selected, only the samples specified in the sample list will be used to affect the parameter.

Steps to set up an Executed Shape:

- Create or edit an existing Expression.
- Click "Playback" to show the lower part of the window.
- Set Type to Tempo.
- Choose "Execute Shape" and click "Select."
- Choose your shape.
- If you want to edit the various scale parameters discussed above, click "Edit".
- Click OK and/or Select until Finale exits the Expression Tool.

Exercise 10.2

Use the same Finale file you used in Exercise 10.1 and set tempos with Expressions at different measures. Also, try the "Execute Shape" to do *accel.*'s and *rit.*'s

 Tempo Tool

The Tempo Tool lets you create or edit measure by measure, or tiny, moment-by-moment tempo fluctuations within the playback of your piece.

In the Tempo Adjustment dialog box, "beats" refers to the beat in the current time signature, rather than assuming a quarter note is the beat.

The measure range defaults to this measure only (instead of through the end of the piece). Most tempo adjustments, except for "swing", should be placed only at the beginning of the area they are to affect.

Tempo data is what you "capture" in Transcription Mode from your real-time performance (by clicking Save Tempo) so that Finale can recreate your tempo changes when it plays back the transcription. In this dialog box, however, you can directly edit the Tempo data for the measure you click.

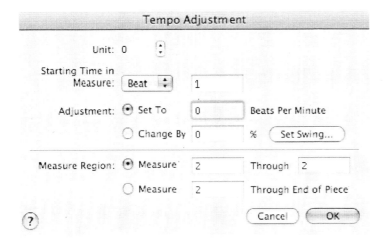

Unit

Indicates the set of tempo-change information. You can have more than one per measure each, starting at a different beat or portion of a beat.

Starting Time in Measure: Beat, EDÚ's

Use this drop-down list to specify whether the tempo change starting point is measured in beats or EDU's (EDU = 1024th of a quarter note). Enter where you want the tempo change to occur, measured in the amount of musical time from the beginning of the measure.

Set to

Sets the tempo to a specific fixed value. Enter the new tempo.

Change by %

Changes the tempo by making it a percentage of the previous tempo. Enter a percentage by which to change.

Set Swing

Creates a swing feel.

Measure Region

Measure__Through__, Measure__Through End of Piece. Specifies for how long this tempo or swing will be in effect

Exercise 10.3

Use the same Finale file you used in Exercise 10.2 and use the Tempo Tool to change the tempo in various places in the music.

Swinging the Eighth Notes

You can use the Tempo Tool to add a swing feel to sections of your music. You can do the same thing with the Playback controls by using Playback Swing which will change your <u>entire</u> piece, whereas the Tempo Tool will affect only certain sections of your piece.

Percent- The amount of swing you want. The higher the percentage number, the later the second eighth note in a swing pair will be. A value of 200 produces a perfect, triplet-feel swing.

Set Swing Ratio
Percent: 200
Duration... 512
?   Cancel   OK

Duration- Allows you to specify what you want to swing. The default is eighth notes (512 EDU's). To swing sixteenth notes use 256 EDU's.

Exercise 10.3:

Use the Tempo Tool to create the following. Does the playback sound different?

No swing: Swing:

Using Playback with Repeats

Until now we have used repeats for display and printing purposes only, but Finale also lets you use the repeats to affect how the music is played.

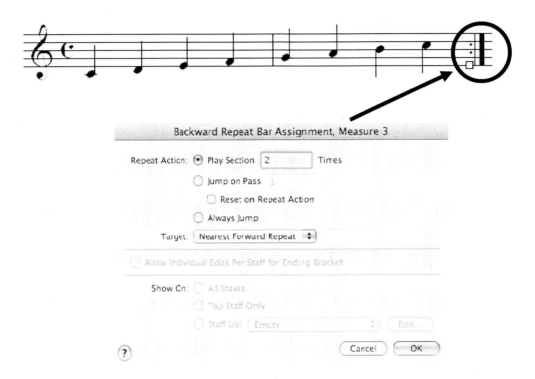

Simple repeats (Backward Repeat Bar Assignment):
After you choose the repeat symbol, the Backward Repeat Bar Assignment box allows you to tell Finale what you want done with the play back.

Repeat Action:
- Play Section *x* Times: Plays the repeated section *x* number of times.

- Jump on Pass: Jumps to the Target measure after the pass value is reached. You can also indicate a range with a hyphen ("2-4") or specific values ("2,3,5").

- Reset on Repeat Action: After playing the music the number of times specified in the Play Section *x* Times or Jump on Pass(es) text boxes this will reset the internal "counter" back to zero and begin counting toward the Total Passes number again. This option could be useful if you're creating nested repeats, and want an inner repeat to be fully executed with each pass of the larger repeated region.

- Always Jump: Will always jump to the target measure each time the playback reaches the repeat barline.

Target Measure:

Specifies the measure Finale will jump to when playback reaches the repeat barline. You can chose from the following options:

- Nearest Forward Repeat: The closest forward repeat barline defined earlier in your score.
- Measure #: The exact measure number to jump to.
- Backward: The number of measures counted backward from the repeat.

Show On:

You can also specify in which staff or staves to show the repeat. You can choose all staves (the default), Top staff only, or define a custom staff list.

Exercise 10.4:

To instruct Finale to play this excerpt correctly, set the playback to **"Play Section 2 Times"** and **"Jump to Nearest Forward Repeat"**.

 Ending Repeat Bar Assignment:

Use this dialog to specify the playback of ending repeats (repeat brackets for numbered endings).

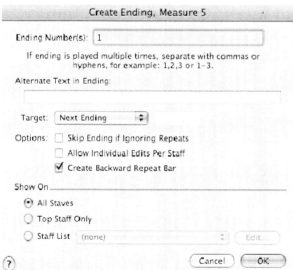

Ending Number(s):

This is where you put the number(s) that you want to appear within the ending bracket. These numbers also affect the playback. You can enter multiple numbers to indicate multiple passes, and Finale will playback the ending accordingly (during playback, after the last pass, Finale will skip over the ending and jump to the specified target). Separate multiple numbers with commas (or a hyphen for number ranges). Finale automatically places a period after a single number if Add Period After Number is checked in Document Options-Repeats.

Alternate Text in Ending: Text entered in this text box will appear within the ending bracket instead. Enter a number sign (#) as a stand-in for the ending number defined above. Text entered in this box does not apply to playback. If you want to combine the Ending Number with other text (for example, "4th time only"), use the number sign (#, which you create by typing shift-3) as a stand-in for the Total Passes number (for example, "#th time only").

Target:

When a target is specified, after playing back the total number of passes (specified in Ending Numbers), Finale will skip from the beginning of the repeat ending measure(s) to the specified target. You can choose from the following targets:

- Next Ending: The next ending in the score.

- Measure #: A specific measure number.

- Forward or Backward: A relative number of measures in that direction.

- Never Skip Ending: Will always be played every time through.

Other Options:

- Skip Ending if Ignoring Repeats: Skips this ending during playback if "Ignore Repeats" is checked in the Playback/Record Options dialog box.

- Create Backward Repeat Bar: Automatically creates a repeat bar after the ending. (It will be assigned to "Always Jump" and have a target of "Nearest Forward Repeat"). Uncheck this box when creating the last ending of a repeated section or if you want to create the Backward Repeat Bar yourself.

Show On:

See the same options for Backward Repeats.

See how easy it is to create fully functional repeat bars.

Exercise 10.5:

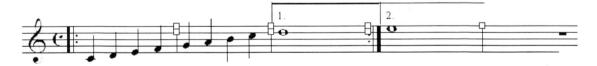

Create the proper playback definition for the example above for the first and second endings:

- Make the first ending: Target =Next Ending and select "Create Backward Repeat Bar."

- Make the second ending with no Target specified.

- Playback the music, making sure it functions correctly.

Text Repeat Assignment:

Use this dialog box to define the playback effect for each text repeat.

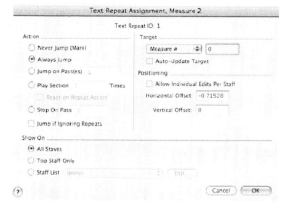

Text Repeat ID: (#): This indicator identifies the text repeat by number.

Action:

- <u>Never Jump (Mark):</u> This places the Text Repeat in your music and has no effect on playback.

- <u>Always Jump:</u> Will always jump to the Target.

- <u>Jump on Passes:</u> Specify the pass(es) you want playback to jump to in the defined target. To indicate multiple passes, separate the pass numbers with commas, or indicate a range with a hyphen (e.g. "2-4").

- <u>Play Section *x* Times:</u> Plays the defined repeated section *x* times.
    - o Reset on Repeat Action: After playing the music the number of times specified in the Play Section *x* Times text boxes, this will reset the internal "counter" back to zero and begin counting toward the Total Passes number again. This option could be useful if you're creating nested repeats, and want an inner repeat to be fully executed with each pass of the larger repeated region.
- <u>Stop on Pass *x*:</u> This halts playback after a certain number of passes. Music **does not** continue playing once a Stop has occurred.
- <u>Jump if Ignoring Repeats:</u> Jumps to the target even if "Ignore Repeats" is checked in the Playback/Record Options dialog box.

Target:
Directs the flow of playback to another measure as follows:
- <u>Text Repeat ID:</u> The assigned ID number of another repeat in your score.
- <u>Measure #:</u> The specific measure number to which the text repeat should direct playback.
- <u>Backward:</u> The number of measures counted **backward** from the measure with the text repeat.
- <u>Forward:</u> The number of measures counted **forward** from the measure with the text repeat.

Auto Update Target:
If this option is checked, the target will update to accommodate measures in the repeated section that have been added, deleted, or inserted.

Show On:
See the same options for Backward Repeats.

Keep in mind that text repeats affect the playback at the end of the measure. Like a repeat bar, these do not cause the music to jump or stop until the measure to which they are attached is played. With this in mind, you may have to assign your text repeats to the previous measure in order for them to function properly.

Exercise 10.6:

Create the following music and correctly define the playback as shown:

- Enter the music below.
- Create the D.S. as a Text Repeat defined to Never Jump (Mark) in the first measure. Remember the Text Repeat ID of the Repeat Assignment screen. You'll need it for step 5.
- Create the Coda symbol defined to Never Jump (Mark). Remember the Text Repeat ID of the Repeat Assignment screen. You'll need it for step 10.
- Create the "To Coda #" in measure 3 and define as "Jump on Passes 2."
- Set the Target to the Text Repeat ID from step 3.
- Create the "D.S. al #" in measure 4 as Always Jump.
  Set the Target to the Text Repeat ID from step 5.
- Play back the piece to be sure you have set the repeats correctly.

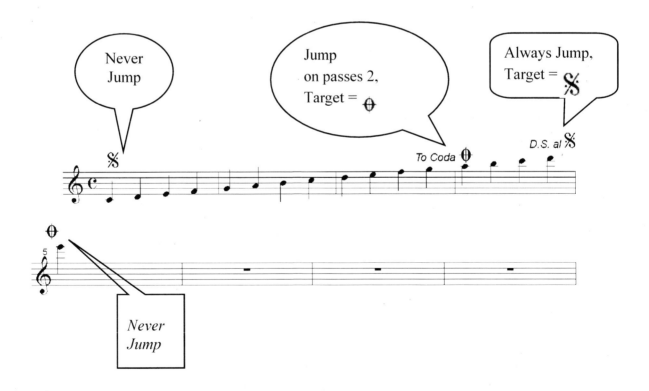

Creating Instruments for Playback

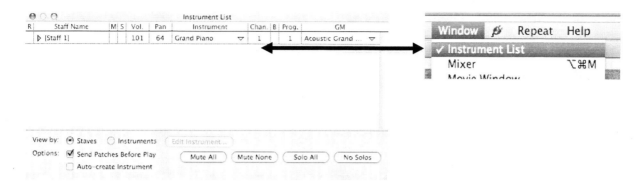

Use this window to control the playback and the instrument assignments (MIDI sounds) of the staves in your score. The easiest way to work is to assign one instrument to each staff. If you need to create a new instrument, click "View by Instrument" and then click "New Instrument." Do Not change the Channel, Bank, or Program settings in the "View by Staves" window. This will change all other instruments assigned to the same MIDI channel.

R (Record)
Click the "R" column to record this instrument when using the HyperScribe Tool.

Staff Name
Click the arrow by the staff name to display the settings for the entire staff, or for each element of the staff. When the arrow points down, you control the playback of the staff as a whole. When the arrow points up, you can individually control the playback of each element of the staff (layers and chords and expressions).

S (Solo)
Click in this column to play back only the staves (or instruments) with a dot in the Solo column.

M (Mute)
Click in this column to mute the staves. These staves will not play.

Volume
The exact volume of this channel (from 0 to 127).

Pan
The exact pan level (left/right) of the channel from 0 to 127. 0 is all the way to the left; 64 is centered; 127 is all the way to the right.

Instrument
Displays the instrument currently assigned to the staff (or staff element). Click the arrow to display the existing instruments available in your score. Select another instrument from the list, or choose None if you don't want the staff to playback at all. You can also choose New Instrument from the list to create another instrument to add to the list.

Chan, B, Prog. (Channel, Bank, Program Change)

Specifies the MIDI Channel, Bank, and Program Change information for the selected instrument, and any staff (or staff element) using that instrument.

GM

Displays the General MIDI descriptive name of the Program number. By clicking on the name, you produce a drop-down list containing all the names. Select the desired GM name to have Finale fill in the matching Program Number.

View by Staves

Displays the settings for each staff of the score in score order. The staff names appear on the left side of the Instrument List.

View by Instruments

Displays the instruments (MIDI sounds) in alphabetical order and indicates which staves use the instrument sound. The Instruments appear on the left side of the Instrument List.

Send Patches Before Play

Determines whether to send patch information set in the Instrument List to the appropriate MIDI device each time you playback.

Auto-create Instrument

Creates a new instrument (assigned to Channel 1, Patch 1) each time a staff is added in the score. This setting is useful if you want to make sure each staff can have different patches or dynamics, or if you want each staff to be assigned to a separate track when you create a MIDI file.

Mute All, Mute None

Click Mute All to turn off the playback of all staves or instruments with a single click. Click Mute None to turn on the playback of all the instruments.

Solo All, No Solos

Click Solo All to set all staves or instruments to solo (play back) with a single click. Click No Solos to turn off the solo of all staves or instruments with a single click.

Edit Instrument

Displays the Instrument Definition dialog box in which you can edit the name, MIDI Channel and Patch number for the selected instrument.

New Instrument (view by Instruments)

Displays the Instrument Definition dialog box in which you can specify a name, MIDI Channel and Patch number for the newly created instrument.

Delete Instrument (view by Instruments)

Deletes the selected instrument name in the Instrument column.

Putting it all together...

Use your own multi-stave Finale file or the score in the *Putting it all together exercise* from chapter 7 and create instruments for each staff. Experiment with creating different instruments based on your own MIDI system until you find a sound you like.

Tools covered in this chapter are listed below:

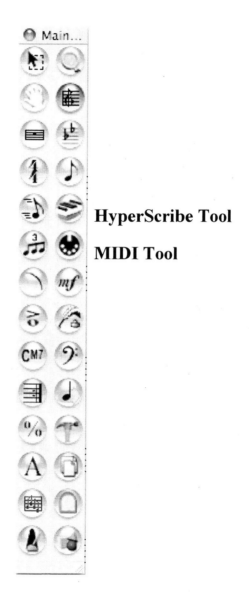

HyperScribe Tool

MIDI Tool

 # HyperScribe® Tool

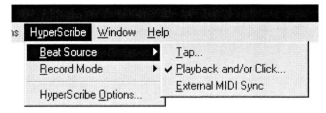

The HyperScribe Tool is one of Finale's real-time transcription tools. You use it to transcribe a live keyboard performance into notation as you play, even onto two staves.

Before you transcribe a real-time performance, there are a few things that Finale needs to know about the music you're about to play. You need to tell Finale whether or not it will be keeping the tempo, and what rhythmic value to use to mark keep the beats.

Beat Source Methods:

I. Tap- You Keep the Beat
- Standard Sustain Pedal
- Nonstandard Sustain Pedal (where the "up" and "down" signals are reversed)
- MIDI Note, Channel
- Other

Listen
Click "Listen", play the note or pedal you want to use for the beat, and Finale will do the rest.

Beat: Tap Equals, EDU's
Click the note duration you would like to use for your tap beat or the EDU value.

Tap States: Select:
If there's a meter or tempo change in your piece, you can switch beat and quantization setups in midstream using Tap States. To return to a single tap/quantization setup, unselect the Tap States checkbox. See Tap States dialog box for more information.

II. Playback and/or Click

Provides a metronome click for the beat and plays any music in existing staves.

III. External MIDI Sync:

Choose External MIDI Sync if you're using HyperScribe to transcribe music being played by an external sequencer or another computer that's equipped to transmit a MIDI Sync signal. Finale will wait for such a signal from the external sequencer, at which point Finale will automatically "sync up" to it, transcribing the music as it goes. No tapping (or even playing) is necessary.

Record Mode:

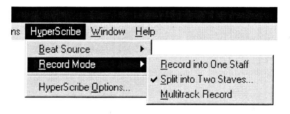

I. Record into One Staff

II. Split into Two Staves

Finale notates your performance onto the staff you click and the staff below it. The notes are split into the two staves according to the note you specify in the Fixed Split Point dialog box.

III. Multitrack Record

Records onto any number of staves or layers of staves simultaneously. Uses the Instrument List's R (Record) column to determine into what staves or layers to record. Finale also uses the Instrument List's RChan (Record Channel) column, which only appears when Multitrack Record is selected, to determine the incoming channel(s) for which the staff or layer is set to record. Click a measure or click the Playback Controls' Record button to start recording; Finale notates the music onto the staves or layers selected for recording.

HyperScribe Options:

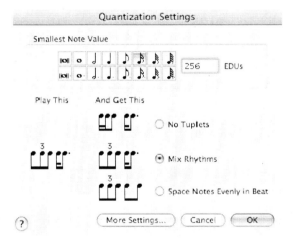

Tie Across Barlines
Determines whether to tie notes into the next measure. For a cleaner transcription, be careful not to hold down notes over the barline you do not want to be tied.

Refresh Screen
Determines whether to keep your screen display current, showing you the notes as you play them.

Show HyperScribe Dialog
Determines whether the HyperScribe dialog box appears when a HyperScribe session is started.

Receive On: All Channels, Only Channel
Determines whether to transcribe MIDI information received on all channels or only on a specific MIDI channel.

Quantize Settings:
The Quantization Settings dialog box allows you to specify the smallest note value to which Finale will quantize input and the type of quantization it will perform, such as allowing or ignoring tuplets.

Smallest Note Value
Select the smallest note value you expect to play from the palette displayed. If the value is not available, type the EDU value in the text box. (One quarter note = 1024 EDU's, so an eighth note triplet is 1024 divided by 3 or 341).

No Tuplets
This option tells Finale that there will be no triplets (or any other tuplets) in your transcription.

Mix Rhythms
This option distinguishes between tuplet and non-tuplet rhythms, based on the timing of the notes within the beat. Needless to say, a Mix Rhythms setting requires you to play accurately enough for the computer to make such distinctions.

Space Notes Evenly in Beat

This option tells Finale to count the number of notes you play during a certain beat, and to notate them on that basis. If you played three notes, no matter how unevenly, they'll be transcribed as a triplet; four notes will appear as sixteenth notes, and so on. These characteristics make Space Notes Evenly in Beat a good setting for swing tunes, because triplets are perfectly transcribed, and all the swung eighth notes are transcribed as normal eighth notes, the correct notation for swing (provided you write "Swing" above the first measure, as a performance indication). If you play only two sixteenths and one eighth note, it will still be transcribed as a triplet.

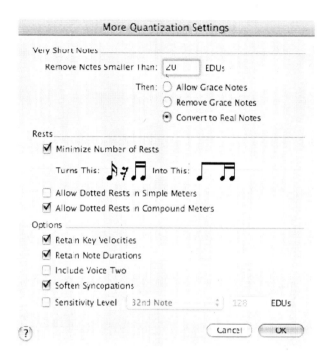

More Quantization Settings:

Very Short Notes:
- Remove Notes Smaller than: _____
- Allow Grace Notes.
- Remove Grace Notes.
- Convert to Real Notes.

Rests:
- Minimize Rests (good if you don't play the notes long enough).
- Allow Dotted Rests in Simple Meters (2/4, 3/4, 4/4, etc.).
- Allow Dotted Rests in Compound Meters (3/8, 6/8, 9/8, etc.).

Options:

- Retain Key Velocities (records how hard you hit the notes).
- Retain Note Durations (records how long you held the note(s) down).
- Include Voice Two.
- Soften Syncopations.
- Sensitivity Level: The number in this text box represents the finest quantization level Finale will use.

Exercise 11.1
Tap Example:

Use HyperScribe Tool with <u>Tap as the Beat Source</u>. You can either use the Sustain Pedal to mark the beats or a MIDI note. Try to play in the following example and see how you do. Press and release your Tap Source (pedal or key) for each beat.

REMEMBER: Since you are marking the beats yourself with the Sustain Pedal or MIDI note, it doesn't matter how fast or slow you play just as long as it's accurate.

If your music isn't transcribing the way that you thought it would, try changing the Quantize Settings as described above.

Click Example:

Use HyperScribe Tool with <u>Click as the Beat Source</u>.

SETUP

Beat Equals: Set to what you want the click to equal. (One click = one quarter note, for example.)

Exercise 11.2

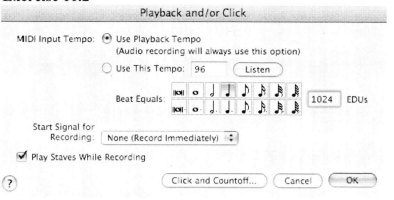

Tempo: Set the tempo by typing in a value or by clicking "Listen" and taping the tempo on your keyboard.

<u>REMEMBER</u>: Since this time Finale is marking the beats, you now must play within the tempo that Finale is beating. If you don't, the music will not transcribe properly.

Play Staves While Recording:
Allows you to hear the music in the other staves.

Start Signal for Recording:
Choose either None (which starts recording as soon as you click a measure) or Any MIDI Data (which starts recording as soon as you press a key).

Click and Countoff:
Gives you other options for counting off measures before recording starts and for choosing the click sound.

Example:

Play/Record each staff separately and have Finale play it back while you record the other staff.

Exercise 11.3

Split Staff Example:

<u>SETUP:</u>

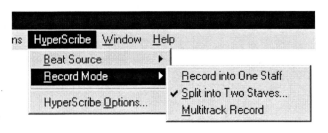

- Set record mode to "Split into Two Staves".

- Set the Split Point either by entering the MIDI Note number or by clicking "Listen" and playing the note on your keyboard. <u>REMEMBER</u>: All notes below this key will appear on the lower staff. For this example, click "Listen" and play a middle C for the split point.

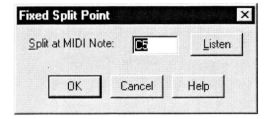

- Use either Tap Beat Source or Click Beat Source and play enter the following example:

Playback Options that Affect Recorded Playback

Once you use HyperScribe to record your music, you not only record the pitches, but also the Key Velocity, exact Note Durations, and any other Continuous Data such as pedaling or Tempo Changes. (All this data can be edited using the MIDI tool discussed later in this chapter). If you want Finale to play back your exact "performance" as when you recorded it, make sure that the above options are selected under the Playback Options menu. If you want Finale to play back quantized version of your music where all the notes are equal, turn off the above options.

The following playback options are available:

- **Play Recorded Key Velocities:** Playback is as loud or as soft as you recorded.

- **Play Recorded Note Durations:** Playback notes are as long or as short as you recorded. Displayed note values are not necessarily what you will hear but show the quantized values of the notes played.

- **Play Recorded Continuous Data:** Playback uses Sustain Pedal, Mod Wheel, etc.

- **Play Recorded Tempo Changes:** Tempos you recorded or created with the Tempo Tool are played.

Exercise 11.3:

Using one of the examples in this chapter that you recorded using the HyperScribe Tool, experiment listening to your piece with the playback options discussed above both on and off.

What is the difference in the performance?
Which sounds better?

HyperScribe-Transcription Mode

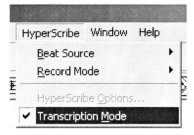

You can use the HyperScribe Tool in a live setting by using Transcription Mode. You play freeform and assign beats and measures after the fact.

Transcription Mode differs from regular HyperScribe in that after you've played your piece, it retains your performance in a graphic sequencer-like window. You can then "transcribe" any part of your performance into real notes in Finale.

The following window can be compared to a mini sequencer and is used to control how Finale transcribes your real-time performances.

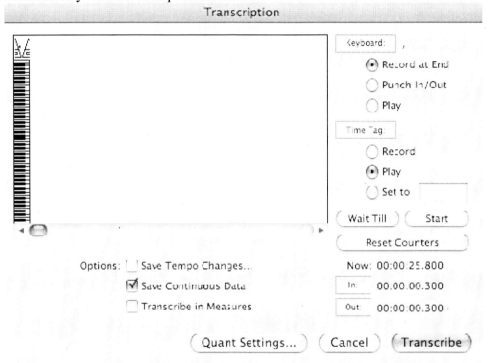

While all of the buttons and menu items may look confusing at first, it is straightforward to use. In general, you first record your performance. Then go back and assign Time Tags where the beats fall. Then tell Finale to assign measure tags. And finally, click "Transcribe" to create your music. On the next few pages is a simplified explanation of how to do a transcription.

Basic steps to using Transcriptions:

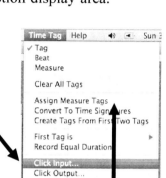

- With the HyperScribe Tool selected, turn on "Transcription" under the HyperScribe Menu.
- Click on the measure where you want to start your transcription.
- Set "Keyboard" to **Record at End**.
- Click **Wait Till.**
- Play your music.
- Click anywhere on the screen to stop recording.
- If you want to play back what you recorded, first set "Keyboard" to **Play** and then highlight the data in the Transcription display area. Then click "**Start.**"
- Tell Finale where the beats go.
- Set up your Click Input source by going under the TimeTag menu and selecting "**Click Input.**"
- Click "**Listen**" and then play the MIDI key you want to use to mark the beats. Then click OK.
- Set "Time Tags" to **Record** (make sure "Keyboard is set to "**Play**").
- Highlight all data in the Display Area.
- Click **Wait Till** and start to tap your Click Source every beat. Make sure you follow the tempo in which you played the music.
- When the music is done, click anywhere to stop recording.
- Select "**Assign Measure Tags**" from under the Time Tag menu. You must do this every time.
- Finally, click **Transcribe** and Finale will convert your performance into notated music.

You might be thinking "If that's all I need to do to create a transcription, why are there so many options and buttons?" If you are only going to enter short and simple sections of music with the HyperScribe Transcription, you might never use most of the Transcription options available to you. They are there to help you start and stop recording at precise locations as well as to create Beat and Measure Tags.

The following is a description of the other HyperScribe Transcription functions:

Display Area:
Displays where the beats occur for the recorded music and displays any music you've recorded. The keyboard helps you identify the pitches of notes in the display area. Each note appears as a horizontal bar: length indicates duration, vertical placement indicates pitch. Use the scroll bar, as needed, to move through the recorded music.

Keyboard:

- **Record at End:** Records new music after any music you've already recorded.

- **Punch In/Out:** Records new music over any music in the selected region.

- **Play:** Plays the music you've already recorded.

Time Tags:
To edit the beats (time tags) in the display, click this word to highlight it.

- **Record:** Records the beats (time tags) you specify by playing.

- **Play:** Plays the metronome click (time tags) you've created.

- **Set to:** Creates evenly spaced beats (time tags) throughout the selected region. Enter the number of beats per minute for the metronome (time tag) click.

Wait Till:
To use a signal (any note or other MIDI event), before recording or playing the music.

Start:
To start recording or playing immediately.

Reset Counters:
To set the time counters to zero (and remove any selection in the display area).

Now:
Indicates the cursor position, in thousandths of a second.

In:
Indicates where to start recording over existing music (the "punch-in" point).

Out:
Indicates where to stop recording over existing music (the "punch-out" point).

Start:
Indicates where to begin recording new music, in thousandths of a second.

Save Tempo Changes...

Determines whether tempo changes (variations in time tag spacing) are stored for playback.

You can save the tempo changes as an Absolute Tempo, a Percent Alteration, or a Percent Alteration with an End of Measure Reset.

Save Continuous Data

Determines whether the recorded continuous data (patch changes, pedaling, pitch bend, and so on) is stored for playback.

Transcribe in Measures

Determines whether the recorded music is transcribed (notated) one measure at a time (by clicking measures in the score).

Quantization. . .

Click this button to display the Quantization Settings dialog box which will affect the accuracy of the transcription (notated outcome).

Transcribe

To transcribe (notate) the music you've recorded.

Even more HyperScribe Transcription options:

(Found under the Time Tag menu when in HyperScribe Transcription mode).

Tag Type:

- Tag: The normal Time Tag. Each tap on a key or pedal lets you specify the position of a beat.

- Beat: Rarely used. It has no effect unless you're using the "Convert to Time Signatures" feature, which creates meter changes in the score based upon your measure and beat taps in the Transcription window. Each Beat Tag you record (after recording normal Time Tags) is represented by a small accent symbol (>) at the top of the Time Tag display area.

- Measure: Only used if the meter changes during the section you're transcribing and you haven't created these meter changes in the score in advance. You need to add this type of tag AFTER you have recorded the normal Tags.

Clear all Tags:
Lets you start over in recording your tags

Assign Measure Tags:
Automatically puts measure tags, based on the time signature, in the score starting with the measure you clicked. You must use this command every time you transcribe music into your score.

Convert To Time Signatures:
Creates time signatures based on the measure tags you created. To use you must first record regular Time Tags. Then you must do a second pass of recording Measure Tags to show Finale how many beats are in each measure.

Create Tags from First Two Tags:
If your first two tags are well placed, this option can create all the remaining tags. Your music must be at a constant tempo and your playing must be accurate for this to be effective.

First Tag is:
The rhythmic value of the first Time Tag you tap. If you've also selected Record Equal Durations, this rhythmic value is assigned to all your taps.

Record Equal Durations:
Tap along on every beat and let Finale do the rest. Tell Finale what the tag is using "First tag is…" (See above).

Click Input:
Allows you to assign what MIDI event is defined as the click. As long as the Keyboard Play option button is selected, and the Time Tag Record option button is selected, Finale interprets a press of any key on MIDI channel 1 as a Time Tag.

Click Output:
Allows you to assign which MIDI note and MIDI channel Finale should use when it plays back the Time Tags.

Align Tags to Notes: Aligns the tags to the closest note. Useful if the notes were slightly off when you recorded the tags.

Exercise 11.7:

Follow the above steps to make a few bars of music, assign tags, and then measure tags. Finally, transcribe your music into printed form.

 # MIDI Tool

The MIDI Tool allows you to edit the actual MIDI data that Finale stores with your music. You can edit the default MIDI data that Finale supplies when you enter notes with the Simple or Speedy Entry Tools or actual performance data that you have recorded with the HyperScribe Tool.

The follow MIDI data can be viewed and edited:

- Key velocities (how hard each note was struck).
- Start and Stop Times (rhythmic information).
- Channel pressure (pressure applied to a key after it's been struck).
- Controller data (pedaling, modulation wheel usage, and so on).
- Pitch bend information.
- Patch change events.

When you click this tool, the MIDI menu appears, containing all the commands you need to increase, decrease, or gradually change any of the above data types. By clicking either on the notes themselves or in the actual MIDI data window, you select which note(s) you want to edit. Then chose how you will edit the data-- You can Set all the values to a specific value, Scale the values, Add to the current values, Alter the current values by a percentage, Limit the values, Alter the Feel, or even Randomize the values.

Example 11.4
Showing key velocities:

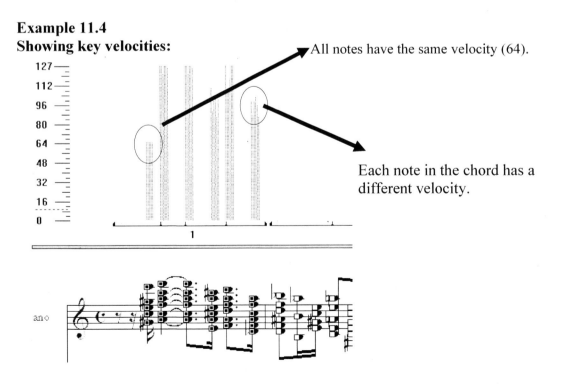

All notes have the same velocity (64).

Each note in the chord has a different velocity.

Example 11.4
Showing note durations:
The vertical bars represent time where the note should begin and end based on the note's written duration. The horizontal bars show where the note actually starts and ends based on the performance data. Therefore, if a note is played early, its horizontal bar will begin before its vertical bar. If a note is held too long, its horizontal bar will extend past the vertical bar. You can edit these start and end times by double clicking on the note and entering the values in EDU's, or by highlighting notes and/or MIDI data and selecting a function under the MIDI menu to set them to a certain value or scale them for example.

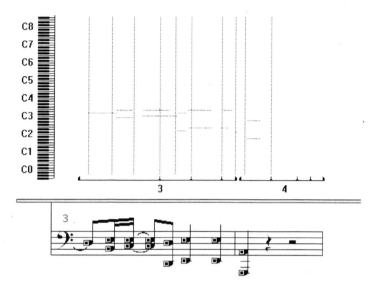

Example 11.5
Showing continuous data (in this case, sustain pedal):

You can work with continuous data in the same way as other MIDI data. First select "Continuous Data..." under the MIDI menu and choose the type of data you want (Controller, Patch Change, Channel Pressure or Pitch Wheel). Then highlight an area in the MIDI window over the notes you wish to change and select a function under the MIDI menu to manipulate or add MIDI data.

Functions to change MIDI data:

- <u>Set To</u>: Sets the values of the specified MIDI data type (velocity, durations, or continuous data) for all selected notes to a single value. To specify pedaling, select the point at which you want the sustain pedal to go down by dragging through a small sliver of the  graph area. Choose Set To, and enter 127. When Finale plays back the music, it will push the pedal "down" at the point you specified. Repeat the process at the point where you want the pedal released, but choose Set To and enter 0 (zero).

  - ○ Applies to:
    - ▪ Key Velocities.
    - ▪ Note Durations (Start - Stop Times).
    - ▪ Continuous Data.
    - ▪ Patches.
    - ▪ Tempo.

- <u>Scale</u>: Allows you to scale the values of the specified MIDI data type (velocity, durations, or continuous data) evenly from one value to another across the selected region. This command is also useful for creating pitch bends. You can scale the MIDI velocity values either from one specified absolute value to another, or from one percentage of the original value to another (from 1% to 100% of the original values, for example).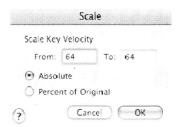

  - ○ Applies to:
    - ▪ Key Velocities.
    - ▪ Note Durations (Start - Stop Times).
    - ▪ Continuous Data.
    - ▪ Tempo.

- <u>Add</u>: Allows you to add (or subtract by adding a negative amount) to the values of the specified MIDI data type (velocity, durations, or continuous data) for all selected notes.

  - ○ Applies to:
    - ▪ Key Velocities.
    - ▪ Note Durations (Start - Stop Times).
    - ▪ Continuous Data.
    - ▪ Tempo.

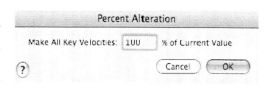

- Percent Alter: Allows you to increase or decrease the values of the specified MIDI data type (velocity, durations, or continuous data) for all selected notes by a percentage of their original values.
  - o Applies to:
    - Key Velocities.
    - Note Durations (Start - Stop Times).
    - Continuous Data.
    - Tempo.

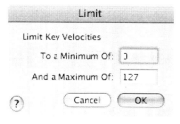

- Limit: Allows you to limit the values of the specified MIDI data type (velocity, durations, or continuous data) for all selected notes to a certain minimum and maximum value. Any notes with values above the maximum you specify will be clipped back to that maximum value; any notes with values below the minimum will be boosted to that minimum value.
  - o Applies to:
    - Key Velocities.
    - Note Durations (Start - Stop Times).
    - Continuous Data.

- Alter Feel: Allows you to add a positive or negative number to the velocities or durations of every note in the selected region. You can target Downbeats, Other Beats, and Backbeats in each measure to receive the alterations. You can specify a different value for each one.
  - o Applies to:
    - Key Velocities.
    - Note Durations (Start - Stop Times).

- Randomize: Allows you to randomly alter the velocity or duration values for all selected notes.
  - o Applies to:
    - Key Velocities.
    - Note Durations (Start - Stop Times).

- <u>Edit MIDI Note:</u> Allows you to set the start and stop times, and the key velocity of a note in one place.

- <u>Play:</u> Plays the displayed music immediately using the captured MIDI data. This command is only available if the MIDI Tool window is open

- <u>Show Selected Notes:</u> Draw lines in the graph area for only notes whose handles are selected. This command is only available if the MIDI Tool window is open.

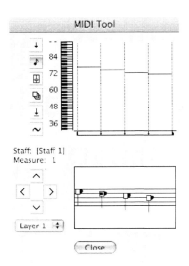

With "Show Selected Notes" Turned OFF

With "Show Selected Notes" Turned ON

- <u>Fit to Time:</u> Allows you to fit the selected measure(s) into a certain amount of time either by slowing them down or speeding them up. You either change the Elapsed Time or the Ending Time of the section. A tempo change will be created to either slow down or speed up your music depending on the values you entered. For example, if you set a New Elapsed Time longer than the one displayed, the music will be slowed down. If you set a New End Time sooner than the one displayed, the music will be sped up to accomplish this.

- <u>Dragging Copies Music:</u> Copies music while dragging (as you would with the Selection Tool).

- <u>Dragging Copies MIDI Data:</u> Copies MIDI data while dragging.

Exercise 11.6
Take one of your existing Finale scores and experiment with changing the <u>Key Velocity</u>, <u>Note Durations</u>, and <u>Continuous Data</u> to see what effect they can have on your play back. Some suggestions would be to scale a pitch bend over a range of measures. Or set different patch changes via the MIDI tool. Experiment with changing note velocity of notes over several measures.

Importing MIDI Files

Finale can directly open any standard MIDI file. Open as you would a regular Finale file, and tell Finale how to transcribe the MIDI data into notes by one of the three options:

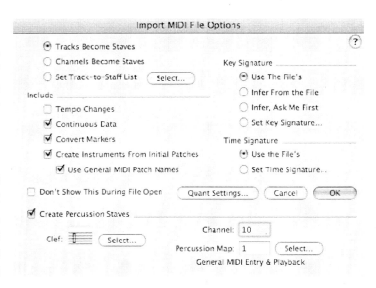

Tracks Become Staves

Places the contents of each MIDI file track into its own staff. Finale will select the treble or bass clef for each staff, based on the register of the music in each track. If the notes have a very wide range, they are split into two staves with different clefs.

Channels Become Staves

Places the contents of each MIDI channel into its own staff, regardless of what tracks they were on in the MIDI file. Clefs are created as needed.

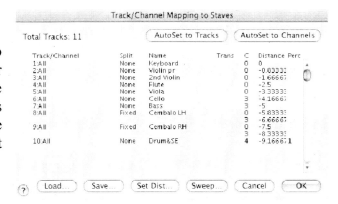

Set Track-To-Staff List

Splits the MIDI file into staves according to any combination of tracks, pitches, or channels that you specify. You can specify the top-to-bottom order of the resulting staves, as well as staff transpositions, clefs, and the distance between staves in the resultant document.

Tempo Changes • Continuous Data • Convert Markers:

You can also include other MIDI data such as Tempo Changes and Continuous Data (such as pedaling, pitch bend, etc.) by clicking the appropriate boxes. In addition, you can convert MIDI file markers to Finale bookmarks.

Setting the Time and Key Signature:

Often the Time Signature and/or Key Signature are/is included in the MIDI file that you are importing. If they are not, you have several options to help you determine the correct time signature and key signature:

Key Signature:

- **Use the File's:** Selects a key signature based on the information, if any, in the MIDI file.
- **Infer from the File:** Selects key signatures based on an analysis of the notes.
- **Infer, ask me first:** Same as above but, asks you to approve each choice.
- **Set Key Signature:** Lets you choose a key signature.

Time Signature

- **Use the File's:** Selects a time signature based on the information, if any, in the MIDI file.
- **Set Time Signature:** Lets you choose a time signature.

Create Instruments from Initial Patches • Use General MIDI Patch Names:

Use these settings to import patch information into Finale's instrument list.

Quant Settings. . .

Use this button to get to the Quantization Settings Dialog box where you can adjust the settings to allow for the most accurate transcription of your MIDI File, being careful of which settings you use. This determines what note values are possible when Finale transcribes the MIDI file to notation. You might need to experiment a little with the quantize settings to get the best results. Having to do a little editing on notes that weren't transcribed properly is par for the course.

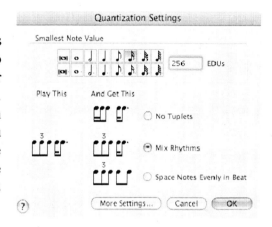

Create Percussion Staves: Channel • Clef • Percussion Map

Use this section to specify the MIDI channel (usually 10), which clef to use, and an optional Percussion Map for Percussion Staves.

Exercise 11.8:

Search the Internet for a standard MIDI file or use your own. An easy way to find a MIDI file is to search by "[name of song].mid". Then try to import your MIDI file. Experiment with the Quantize settings to get the best possible conversion.

Exporting MIDI Files

Finale can easily export MIDI files. To export your music as a standard MIDI file, chose Save As... under the File menu and then select "MIDI File." Then tell Finale what type of MIDI file you would like to create. The three available types are detailed below:

Export MIDI File Options

MIDI File Type:
- ● Format 1 – All Instruments Saved to Separate Tracks
- ○ Format 0 – All Instruments Saved into a Single Track
- ○ Tempo Map

☑ Save Bookmarks as Markers
☐ Don't Show This During File Save As

Cancel   OK

- **Format 1:** Creates separate tracks for each staff assigned to a different instrument.

- **Format 0:** Saves all staves to one track.

- **Tempo Map:** Creates a tempo map only, and ignores any music in the staves.

- **Save Bookmarks as Markers:** Determines whether to convert Finale bookmarks to sequencer markers in the MIDI file.

Exercise 11.9:

Take one of your existing Finale files and save it as a standard MIDI file as mentioned above. Open the resulting MIDI file in your sequencer program or internet browser. Does it sound the same as in Finale?

Putting it all together...

- Experiment with the HyperScribe tool so that you become proficient in entering music by playing it in real time or in transcription mode.

- Experiment with importing MIDI files that you can find on the internet to Finale. Make sure you are able to properly set the quantize amount so that the music is correctly transcribed.

Chapter 12
Advanced Audio

Studio View

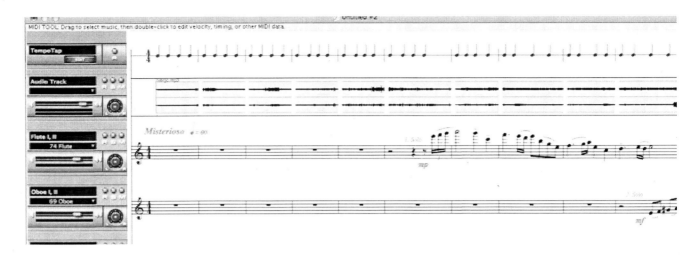

In addition to Page View and Scroll View which we read about earlier, there is a third view called "Studio View." This view is designed for viewing and real-time control while auditioning playback. You can also add an audio track, load audio files, and record audio.

In Studio View, each staff in your piece is displayed along with controls for volume, pan, and program change, as well as mute, solo, and record. These can be adjusted in real-time as you listen to your music. There is also an additional staff called "TempoTap" above the top staff. This staff displays the current main beat duration specified by the time signature.

Instrument Name

MIDI Patch and Name

Volume Slider

Playback Level

Record, Solo, Mute

Pan (Left/Right) Knob

Creating an Audio Track:

To add an Audio Track to your file, select "Audio Track → Add Audio Track" from the MIDI/Audio Menu. This will add a blank audio track to your score in the second from the top position. (The TempoTap track is always at the top of the Studio View.)

Importing an Audio File:

Once you have created an Audio Track in your piece, you can import an audio file to be played on the track. Choose Audio Track → Load Audio... from the MIDI/Audio menu and choose the file you wish to import.

Note: There can be only one audio file per audio track, so you may need to edit your audio file outside of Finale if you want more than just one track to playback.

The Audio Clip Attributes Menu allows you to customize the point in your score where you would like the audio to begin playing. You can also playback only a part of the clip by specifying the start and end points. All the options are detailed below:

- <u>Start in Score:</u> The measure and beat you would like the audio clip to begin playback.

- <u>Repeat:</u> The number of times to repeat the clip.

- <u>Start in Clip:</u> Where in the clip to begin playback. 0 (zero) is the beginning of the clip 00:00:10:000 is 10 seconds after the beginning of the clip.

- <u>End in Clip:</u> Where in the clip to end playback. 00:00:24:000 is 24 seconds after the beginning of the clip. You can also click the "Set to End" button to specify that you want to play out to the end of the clip.

- <u>Display Unit:</u> You can choose time measurements (hours | minutes | seconds | milliseconds) or samples. Note: the total number of samples in your clip depends on the sample rate of the recording. If you imported a CD quality audio file sampled at 44.1 KHz, then there will be 44,100 samples per second of your audio. Conversely, if the sample rate is 22 KHz, there will be 22,000 samples per second of audio.

Recording an Audio File:

If you don't want to import an Audio File, you can record one right in Finale. Select the Record button on Audio track staff in Studio View to mark it for recording.

Or, you can click the red arrow next to the Audio Track in the "R" column in the Instrument List to make the track armed for recording.

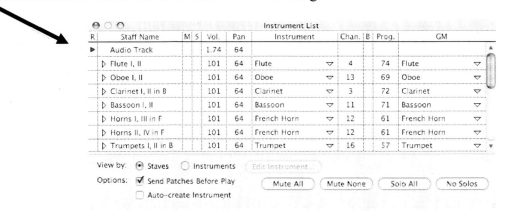

Finally, click the red dot on the Playback Controls to start recording.

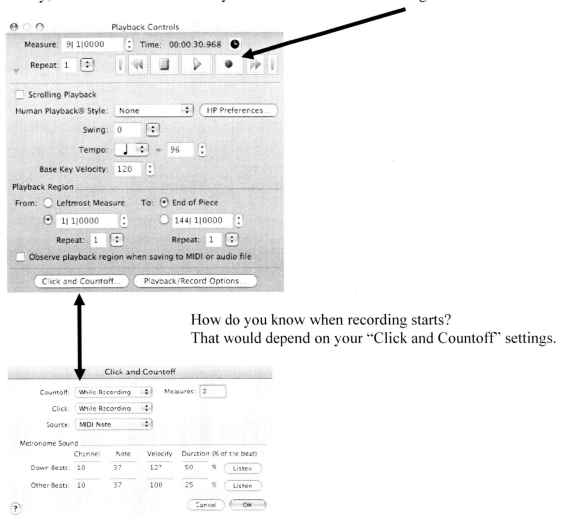

How do you know when recording starts?
That would depend on your "Click and Countoff" settings.

Here you may want to change the Countoff setting to give yourself some time to feel the tempo and get ready to record. In the example above, Finale counts off two measures before starting to record. Finale will also playback the metronome click sound while recording. This may not be what you want if it can be heard in your music.

The Mixer

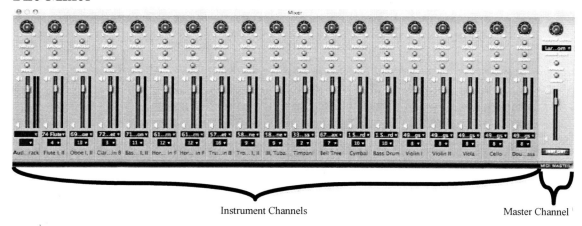

Instrument Channels   Master Channel

The Mixer is very similar to Studio View since it contains playback controls for every staff in your piece. Each channel of the mixer includes the same Pan Knob, Mute/Solo/Record buttons, Volume Slider, Level Indicator, and Patch information that is shown in Studio View. The Mixer, however, gives you more of a landscape view of your entire orchestra, similar to what you might see if you were at a real mixer.

In addition to channels for each staff, the Mixer contains a master set of controls. The master controls can be used to adjust the volume and reverb of the overall output, much like the master controls on a conventional mixer. All settings defined in the mixer are post-processed and applied over the top of MIDI data that already exists in the score including MIDI Tool data, Human Playback data, and/or expressions and articulations defined for playback. In other words, the mixer doesn't change the contour of the playback, only the overall output or the staff relationship. Note: Although the mixer displays separate controls for each staff, only staves of unique MIDI channels can be adjusted independently.

The Master control has another function—adding Reverb to your music. The reverb dial controls the overall amount of decay, or length of time a sound persists after being released. This dial applies to the overall output. Click and drag this dial clockwise to increase the reverb effect or counterclockwise to decrease the reverb effect.

You can also change the type of reverb used in your music by changing the Room Size. This setting has the effect of simulating a room's size to make your music sound as though it is being performed in a small room, concert hall, or anything in-between. The dropdown menu has different room sizes varying from none, medium room, large room, medium hall, large hall, and plate.

The controls on the Master control such as solo, mute, and volume, affect the playback of your entire score. Pressing Mute will silence all staves, while pressing Solo will solo all staves. The volume slider controls the overall volume of your entire piece making all instruments louder or softer proportionately. There is also an Instrument List button to easily bring up the instrument list to make changes.

Finale for Composers

Using Audio Units and VST Instruments

One of Finale strongest points has become its ability to create professional sounding scores with little or no work through Audio Units (AU) on the Mac and VST Instruments on the PC.

Audio Units (AU) and Virtual Studio Technology (VST) are interfaces for integrating software audio synthesizers with music software such as Finale. They both use Digital Signal Processing to simulate traditional recording studio hardware with software. There are other AU and VST plug-ins available that also work with Finale. But since Finale comes with the Garritan Instruments for Finale, this will be the one covered here.

The setup to configure which MIDI source to use is a little different on PC's and Mac's so I will show each one.

Step 1:

The first thing you need to do is tell Finale that you don't want to use MIDI (either its own Software Synth, your sound card, or an external MIDI setup). On both the PC and Mac, this is done under the MIDI/Audio menu. Choose either "Play Finale Through Audio Units" or "Play Finale Through VST" depending on which OS you are running:

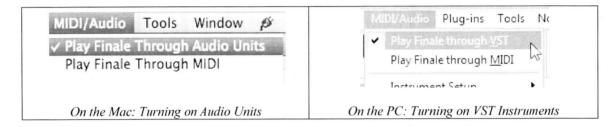

| *On the Mac: Turning on Audio Units* | *On the PC: Turning on VST Instruments* |

Step 2:
Setup the instruments.

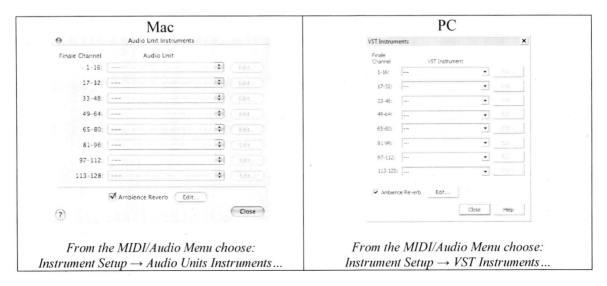

Mac	PC
From the MIDI/Audio Menu choose: *Instrument Setup → Audio Units Instruments...*	*From the MIDI/Audio Menu choose:* *Instrument Setup → VST Instruments...*

Step 3:
Assign your Audio Units or VST instruments to ranges of MIDI channels.

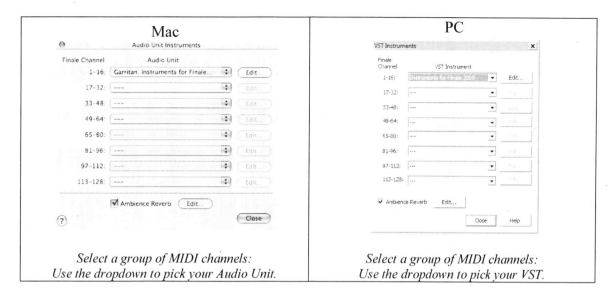

Mac	PC
Select a group of MIDI channels: *Use the dropdown to pick your Audio Unit.*	*Select a group of MIDI channels:* *Use the dropdown to pick your VST.*

In the old days, you had only 16 MIDI channels to work with and that was it. Now you can access up to 128 different MIDI channels. These are still grouped in ranges of 16 MIDI channels, but you can assign each group of 16 to a different Audio Unit or VST Instrument. If you have Audio Units or VST Instruments from other programs, they will also appear in the dropdown menu.

Step 4:
Click "Edit…" and start to assign instruments to MIDI channels.

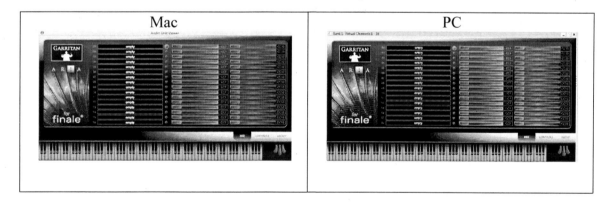

From this point, the creation of instruments is the same for PC's and Mac's.

Anatomy of the Aria Player

The Aria Player for Finale allows you to assign Finale's included Garritan instruments to Finale channels. It also displays the range of each instrument, its keyswitches, and allows you to make adjustments to the properties of the instrument sound.

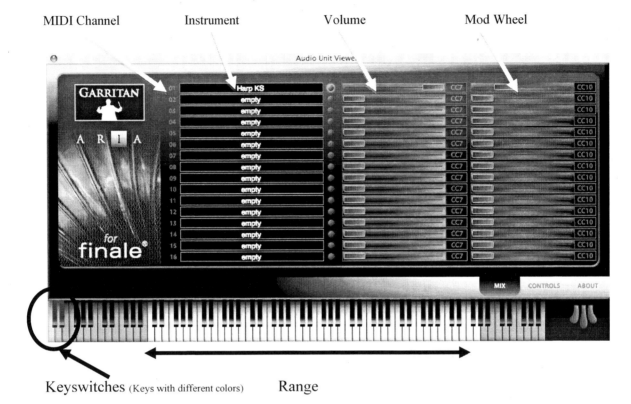

Keyswitches (Keys with different colors)   Range

Note:

The Aria player only shows MIDI channels 1-16. So where are channels 17-128? If you are using bank 17-32, channel 17 is Aria 1; channel 18 is Aria channel 2; and so on. You can think that the first MIDI channel in the group is always MIDI channel 1, the second channel in the group is always MIDI channel 2 and so on. Or, use the simple chart below. Find your MIDI channel and then go to the last column on the left to find the Aria MIDI channel.

1	17	33	49	65	81	97	113
2	18	34	50	66	82	98	114
3	19	35	51	67	83	99	115
4	20	36	52	68	84	100	116
5	21	37	53	69	85	101	117
6	22	38	54	70	86	102	118
7	23	39	55	71	87	103	119
8	24	40	56	72	88	104	120
9	25	41	57	73	89	105	121
10	26	42	58	74	90	106	122
11	27	43	59	75	91	107	123
12	28	44	60	76	92	108	124
13	29	45	61	77	93	109	125
14	30	46	62	78	94	110	126
15	31	47	63	79	95	111	127
16	32	48	64	80	96	112	128

What is a Keyswitch?

If you are an experienced Garritan instrument user, you are probably familiar with the concept of keyswitches.

A keyswitch is a MIDI note outside the normal range of the instrument that triggers a different playing technique for a Garritan instrument — for instance, pizzicato on a violin, or harmonics on a harp.

If you take a closer look at Human Playback Preferences, you can see how keyswitches actually work. For example, when Finale encounters a *pizzicato,* it will execute keyswitch (MIDI note F-2) which) turns on the pizzacato.

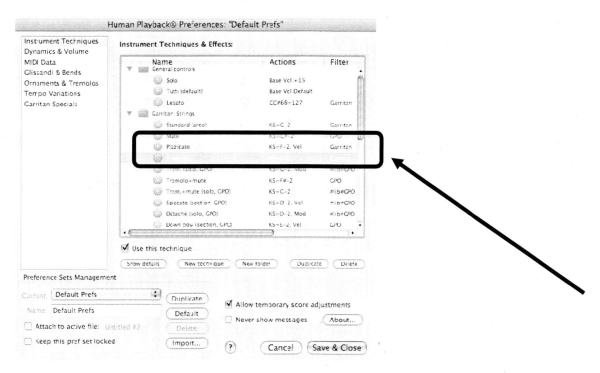

Before keyswitches, you had to do a patch change from an arco string patch to pizzicato string patch or set up another staff that was only used for pizzicato notes. Fortunately, those days are gone and you no longer have to do any extra work to trigger Garritan keyswitches - Human Playback does it all for you.

Note: Make sure you have Human Playback turned on to get all of the benefits of automatic keyswitches.

Assigning Instruments to MIDI channels

Once you have assigned MIDI channels to all your instruments, it's an easy task to assign instruments to them in the Aria player:

1. Find the MIDI channel you want to assign an instrument to and click the word "empty" next to it.

2. A dropdown menu will appear where you can navigate though the families of instruments until you find the exact one you want.

3. If you want to audition the instrument before you commit it to your piece, use the piano keyboard at the bottom of the screen to play a few notes or use your own MIDI keyboard.

4. Be aware that there are several different versions of the same instrument. Flutes, for example, have Flute Player 1, Flute Player 2, Flute Player 3, Flute Solo, and even Piccolo Solo. Using different versions of the same instrument can make your music sound even more realistic as each player will add his/her own nuances to the playback.

Other Controls:

If you want to further customize the playback, click the Controls tab in the lower right of the Aria Player to display some further options.

Porta(mento):
The amount of sliding between notes. Woodwinds, Brass, and Strings have this option. Piano, Harp, and other tuned percussion do not.

Length:
Adjusts the duration of notes. The greater this value, the longer the note will continue to play after the key has been released or the note stops playing.

VAR1:

This controller allows you to introduce random variability in intonation. This can make a big difference, especially in fast passages where real players almost never achieve accurate intonation from note-to-note.

VAR2:

This controller allows you to introduce random variability in timbre.

The two variability controllers can go a long way toward eliminating the dreaded "machine gun" effect of rapid repeated notes. Proper application of the VAR controls can also help the user create convincing double and triple tongued passages in the brass.

ModWhl:

This knob controls the Modulation Wheel controller.

Making your music sound like it's being performed at Carnegie Hall: Ambience Reverb

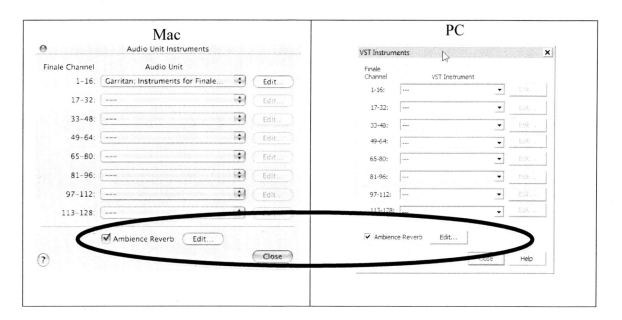

To turn on Ambience Reverb, click the check mark in the Audio Unit Instruments or VST Instruments Setup window as shown above.

To change the quality and parameters of the reverb, click the "Edit…" button.

Again there are differences between the PC and Mac versions of the Ambience Reverb:

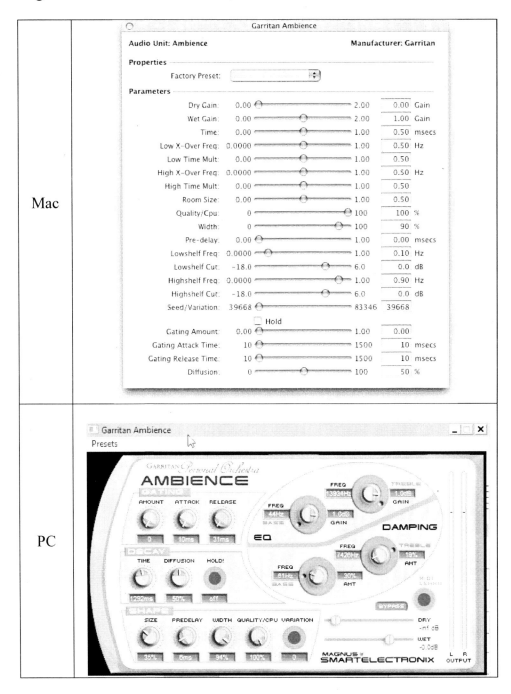

Factory Preset: Start here and pick a room type/size. You might be happy with the results or you can use this as a starting point to further customize the space. The following are some of the customized spaces in Ambience Personal Orchestra Edition.

Ballroom 1	*Ballroom 1*	*Ballroom 2*	*Parlor*
Cathedral	*Piano Hall 1*	*Church*	*Piano Hall 2*
Concert Hall 1	*Recital Hall 1*	*Concert Hall 2*	*Recital Hall 2*
Jazz Club 1			

Although the PC and Mac versions of the Ambiance Reverb look very different, they both have basically the same set controls. The PC version layout is a little more intuitive than the Mac version.

Explanation of Controls for the Mac Version:

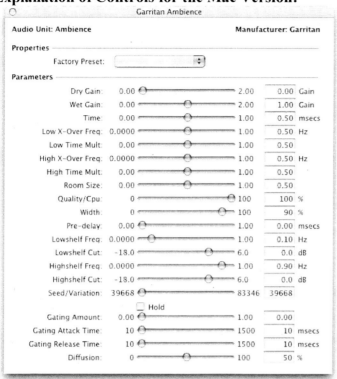

Dry Gain:
Dry always refers to the unprocessed or original sound. This control is the amount of the original sound you want in the resulting reverb.

Wet Gain:
Wet always refers to the processed or affected sound. This control is the amount of the resulting reverb you want in the mix.

Time:
This is the length of the reverb. You might also think of it as the decay, i.e. how long it takes for the reverb reflections to fade away into silence.

Low X-Over Frequency/Low Time Multiplier/
High X-Over Frequency/High Time Multiplier:
These controls allow you to put equalizer effects on the reverb. They can be useful for cutting away bass that can otherwise make the reverb sound muddy. They can also help to simulate the roll-off in response at high frequencies characteristic of most concert halls.

Room Size:
This allows you to change the size of the virtual room in which the reverb will occur. For interesting effects, try a long reverb time in a small room.

Quality/CPU:
This knob allows you to trade reverb quality for CPU usage. High quality = high CPU usage. If there is too much CPU demand on your machine, try turning down the quality.

Width:
Think of this as the distance between the left and right speakers. 0% is no distance between the speakers, while 100% is fill distance between the left and right speakers for full stereo sound.

Pre-delay:
Controls the amount of time between the direct sound and the first of the reverb reflections. It is pre-delay that defines our perception of the size of the room.

Lowshelf Frequency/
Lowshelf Cut/
Highshelf Frequency/
Highshelf Cut:
These commands affect how the reverb's character develops over time as it decays. Use it to control the decay time of bass and treble.

Speed/Variation:
The Variation dial can create a new variant of the same room. If there is some annoying echo or ringing in the reverb that bugs you, adjust this control until you find a desirable variation.

Gating Amount/
Gating Attack Time/
Gating Release Time:
These controls affect how the reverb follows the dynamics of the audio input and can generate some interesting effects.

Diffusion:
This control has a subtle effect on the sound, especially noticeable with small room sizes.

Explanation of Controls for the PC Version:

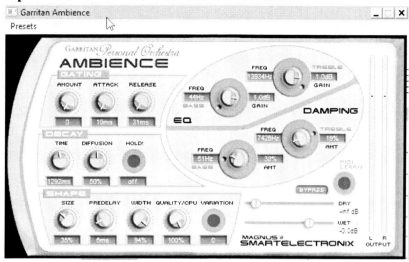

Gating Section: Amount, Attack, Release:

These controls affect how the reverb is affected by the dynamics. The *Amount* is the level that the audio must reach to open the *Gate* or turn on the reverb effect. The *Attack* is the time it takes after the *Amount* value is reached to open the *Gate*. The *Release* is the time it takes to close the *Gate* after the audio has fallen below the *Amount* value.

Decay: Time, Diffusion, Hold:

The *Time* is the length of the reverb. You might also think of it as the decay, i.e. how long it takes for the reverb reflections to fade away into silence. *Diffusion* has a subtle effect on the sound, especially noticeable with small room sizes. The *Hold* button will freeze the reverb at its current sound, holding it indefinitely until you press it again.

Shape: Size, Pre-delay, Width, Quality/CPU, Variation:

- *Size* is the size of the virtual room in which the reverb will occur. For interesting effects, try a long reverb time in a small room.
- *Pre-delay* This controls the amount of time between the direct sound and the first of the reverb reflections. It is pre-delay that defines our perception of the size of the room.
- *Width* can be thought of as the distance between the left and right speakers. 0% is no distance between the speakers, while 100% is full distance between the left and right speakers for full stereo sound.
- *Quality/CPU* This knob allows you to trade off reverb quality for CPU usage. High quality = high CPU usage. If there is too much demand on your CPU, try turning down the quality.
- *Variation* can create a new variant of the same room. If there is some annoying echo or ringing in the reverb that bugs you, adjust this control until you find a desirable variation.

EQ:

These controls allow you to put equalizer effects on the reverb. They can be useful for cutting away bass that can otherwise make the reverb sound muddy.

Damping:
The Damping section affects how the reverb's character develops over time as it decays. Use it to control the decay time of bass and treble.

Dry:
Dry always refers to the unprocessed or original sound. This control is the amount of the original sound you want in the resulting reverb.

Wet:
Wet always refers to the processed or affected sound. This control is the amount of the resulting reverb you want in the mix.

Exporting Audio Files

Once you have created all your Audio Units or VST Instruments, you're only a click away from exporting a CD ready audio file of your music.

From under the File menu, click "Export to Audio File..."

You then have the option to save your music as an AIFF on Mac's, WAVE on PC's and MP3 on both PC's and Mac's.

Note: Compressed files (MP3's) are not supported when using Audio Unit or VST Instruments. You can only used uncompressed AIFF or WAVE file formats in these cases. In you need an MP3 when using AU's or VST's, create an AIFF or WAVE file and then convert it through another means such as i-Tunes. Either way, you will get the best sound quality when using uncompressed file formats but the file sizes will be much larger.

Putting It All Together:

- Find a multi-staff example that uses a few different instruments.

- You can use an exercise which you may have already done from this book or enter your own score.

- Assign a Human Playback style to it.

- Assign appropriate instruments to each staff using AU or VST instruments.

- Finally, export the music as an audio file to share with your friends.

Tools covered in this chapter are listed below:

Selection Tool

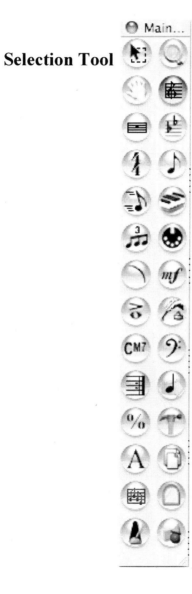

Plug-Ins

Plug-Ins are some of the most powerful and time saving tools in Finale. They are in essence "mini-programs" that allow you to quickly perform tasks that might take many steps, or which extend Finale's functionality. The program comes with many useful Plug-Ins. In addition, there are third-party Plug-Ins also available. And, you can write your own Plug-Ins if you really want to get involved.

Depending on whether you are using the Mac or PC version of Finale, you will have a different set of Plug-Ins. You may or may not have all of the Plug-Ins described here. Also, on Mac's, the Plug-Ins are found under the little plug icon in the menu bar 🔌 . On PC, they are found under the "Plug-Ins" menu.

As you can tell from all of the descriptions of the Plug-Ins on the next several pages, the Plug-Ins range from the simple to the quite complex. A whole book could be written just explaining the details of each Plug-In. Instead of going into too much detail explaining each Plug-In, I have chosen to briefly describe each. If you see one that would be of benefit to you, you can learn more about it from the Finale Users Manual.

All the Plug-Ins work basically the same way—select a portion of your score usually with the Selection Tool, go to the Plug-In menu and chose your Plug-In. If the Plug-In requires any additional input, you will be presented with a list of the appropriate options.

The Plug-In menu can also be customized. Create sub-folders in the Finale/Plug-Ins folder located on your hard drive and copy or move your Plug-Ins to these folders. (See how the Plug-Ins are organized in the graphic at the top of this page). For example, you can move often-used Plug-Ins into the "My Favorite Plug-Ins" folder or create a folder named "Transpositions" to hold Plug-Ins that deal with helping you transpose music.

Expressions:

- **<u>Auto-Dynamic Placement</u>**: Places dynamics automatically in your score based on the MIDI key velocities associated with each dynamic.

- **<u>Create Tempo Marking</u>**: Create tempo markings as expressions and set their playback features for the selected measures.

FinaleScript™:

- **FinaleScript™: Palette:** Opens the FinaleScript Palette, which allows you to choose, edit, or manage scripts.

- **Options:** Choose this option to open the FinaleScript Options dialog box.

- **[Script List]:** You can add scripts to this menu for easy access by checking Show In Menu in the Script Editor dialog box.

Lyrics

- **Auto Slur Melismas:** Scans your document for lyric syllables that carry over two or more pitches and adds slurs accordingly.

- **Clear Lyric Positioning:** Clears any individual positioning of lyrics for the selected lyrics.

- **Extract Lyrics:** Saves all lyrics found in the Edit Lyrics dialog box to a file.

Measures

- **Automatic Barlines:** Automatically adds double-barlines before every key change and a final barline at the end of the piece.

- **Clear Measure # Positioning:** Clears all individual positioning of measure numbers in the selected region.

- **Create Coda System:** Automatically adds a gap between measures in order to create an independent coda system on the same line. Select the measure that you want the Coda to start on and select the Plug-in.

Before creating a Coda section which starts in measure 6.

After clicking on measure 6 and using the "Create Coda System" Plug-in.

- **Easy Measure Numbers:** Places measure numbers over a region of the score.

- **Merge Measures:** Combines two measures into a single measure automatically. Measure numbering and time signature are updated accordingly.

- **Mid-measure Repeats:** Automatically encloses a region (including partial measures) with repeat barlines.

An example of a mid-measure repeat.

- **Number Repeated Measures:** Places small measure attached expression numbers over any repeated measures in the selected region.

- **Split Measure:** Divides a measure over a system break. Measure numbering is also updated correctly.

Miscellaneous

- **Change Fonts:** Globally changes the font for Text blocks, Staff names, Group names, and Lyrics — all at once and separately for verse, chorus, and section.

- **Command Line:** Note entry from a command line.

- **Count Items:** Counts various items in your score such as measures, notes, and articulations. Useful if you want to charge clients by the note or to count the total number of notes in your piece.

Note, Beam, and Rest Editing

- **Patterson Plug-Ins Lite:** These Plug-Ins are a sample of the Patterson Plug-In Collection. They include Patterson Beams, which adjust both stem length and beam angles based on the staff positions of the notes and the number of notes in the beam. They also have Beam Over Barlines, which allows for easy beaming across barlines.

- **Cautionary Accidentals:** Adds cautionary accidentals in various forms to your document including accidentals displayed on all notes.

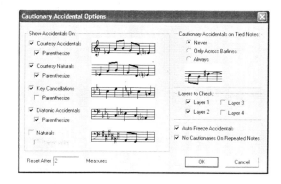

- **Change Noteheads:** Changes the noteheads for the notes in the selected region.

- **Change to Default Whole Rests:** Changes all the whole rests in the selected region to Default whole rests.

- **Change to Real Whole Rests:** Changes all the Default whole rests in the selected region to real whole rests.

- **Check Region for Durations:** Checks the selected region for any measures that have too many or too few beats.

- **Classic Eighth Beams:** Beams eighth notes in the selected region in groups of 4 when in Common Time.

- **Flat Beams:** Flattens all the beams in the selected region.

- **Flat Beams (Remove):** Restores all beams flattened with Speedy Entry in the selected region.

- **Ledger Lines (Hide):** Hides all ledger lines in the selected region.

- **Ledger Lines (Show):** Restores any hidden ledger lines in the selected region.

- **Midline Stem Direction:** Changes the direction of stem for the note on the centerline of the staff to match the stem direction of the previous note.

- **Move Rests:** Moves rests in the selected region to a specified location.

- **Notes and Rests (Hide):** Hides all the notes and rests in the selected region.

- **Notes and Rests (Show):** Shows all hidden entries in the selected region.

- **Resize Noteheads:** Resizes specified voices in the selected layer of a multi-voice staff.

- **Rhythmic Subdivisions:** Subdivides the notes in the selected region by the specified amount, either by a division (such as in half) or to a selected subdivision of the beat such as eighth notes.

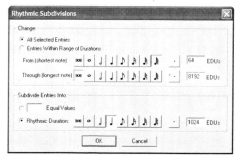

- **Single Pitch:** Changes all the notes in the selected region to the specified pitch.

- **Slash Flagged Grace Notes:** Slashes all the flagged grace notes in the selected region.

- **Slash Flagged Grace Notes (Remove):** Removes the slashes of all the flagged grace notes slashed in Speedy Entry in the selected region.

- **Voice 2 to Layer:** Moves notes and rests in voice 2 to the selected.

Playback

- **Apply Human Playback:** Applies a Human Playback style, or specific elements of Human Playback to a region of your document.

Scoring and Arranging

- **Composer's Assistant:** These Plug-Ins from OpenMusic provide compositional manipulation of chords and melodies.

- **Chord Morphing:** Generates a variety of smooth between-chord transitions.

- **Chord Realization:** Generates four-part realizations of a triad based on the major key and scale degree specified.

- **Chord Reordering:** Finds new placement options for chords.

- **Chord Splitting:** Creates subsets of the original chord.

- **Common Tone Transposition:** Creates a series of transpositions of the chord where one note is equal to one note of the original chord.

- **Frequency Modulation Chord Generator:** Generates a series of chords with increasing complexity and texture.

- **Melodic Morphing:** Creates a melodic transition from one melody to another.

- **Rhythm Generator:** Creates up to six staves of percussion to accompany your score.

- **Tie Common Notes:** Inserts a tie between any two successive notes if the notes have the same pitch.

- **Virtual Fundamental Generator:** Gives you the appropriate "root" for any selected group of chords.

- **Add Cue Notes:** Places cue notes in any number of staves.

- **Band-in-a-Box Auto-Harmonizing:** Takes a selected melody line with chord symbols and outputs a harmonized melody in dozens of musical styles.

- **Canonic Utilities:** Transforms the selected region using inversion, retrograde, transpositions, or a combination of the above. You can also use this Plug-In to apply accidentals to all the notes in a selected region, remove accidentals in the selected region, or remove ties in the selected region.

- **Check Range:** Verifies that the staff you have selected is within the range of a specified instrument or voice. There are different ranges for beginning, intermediate, and advanced players.

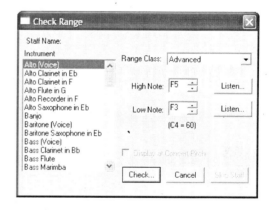

- **Chord Analysis:** Generates chord symbols by analyzing existing notation. This Plug-in works much like the One-Staff Analysis and Two-Staff Analysis options under the chord menu, but for any region of measures selected with the Selection Tool.

- **Drum Groove:** With this Plug-In, easily compose unique rhythms and percussion parts.

- **Find Parallel Motion:** Analyzes the selection for parallel fourths, fifths, and octaves between voices, layers, and staves and offers you the choice to fix them.

- **Find Range:** the highest and lowest notes in the selected region.

- **Global Staff Attributes:** Changes the Staff Attributes and Group Attributes for a number of staves or groups at a time, including changing the font for selected Staff and Group names.

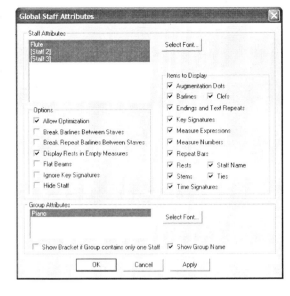

- **Latin Percussion:** Automatically creates authentic Latin Percussion rhythm section notation, with a variety of styles from which to choose.

- **Piano Reduction:** Condenses the selected staves into a piano grand staff at the bottom of the staff system.

- **Score System Divider:** Automatically adds system separation marks between systems in a score.

- **Rhythm Section Generator:** Generates a jazz accompaniment (piano, bass, and drum set parts) for an existing melody with chord symbols.

- **Smart Cue Notes:** Searches for cue note opportunities throughout a document and adds them automatically.

- **Smart Page Turns:** Intelligently edits the pagination of an entire part to avoid awkward page turns.

- **Split Point:** Changes the split point between the two staves of a piano grand staff over the selected region.

- **Update Groups and Brackets:** Edits groups and brackets *en mass* after a document has been optimized.

- **Vertical Collision Remover:** Automatically reformats the vertical positioning of staves, systems, and instrument groups to avoid collision of notes, articulations, smart shapes, and other items.

Third Party Plug-Ins

In addition to these Plug-Ins, newer versions of Finale also come with a sample of the following TG Tools Plug-In collection:

Handbell Used Chart:

Creates a 'handbells used' chart automatically based on all pitches discovered in a region selected with the Selection Tool. The chart can be a single treble clef staff or a grand staff. The chart can be added to the beginning of the document, as is standard practice for handbell scores.

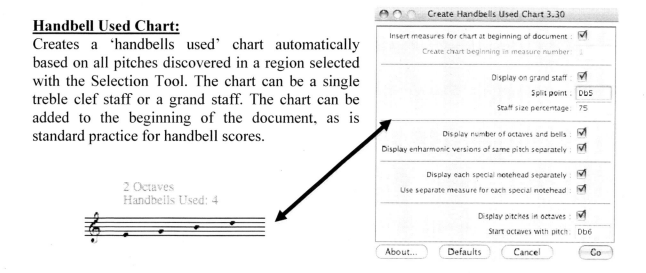

Align/Move Dynamics:

Vertically aligns dynamics, including expressions, and hairpin crescendos.

is adjusted to:

Easy Harmonics:
Searches for intervals of a perfect fourth or third, and turns the upper note into a diamond.

before ...

and after Harmonics automation with all theoretical harmonics selected:

or

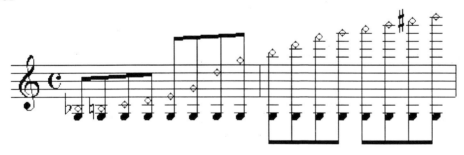

Here, only fourths were selected:

>>>

Modify Rests:

Performs a variety of changes to the duration and appearance of rests for a region of your document. This Plug-in can be use to split, simplify, or shift rests. You can also split notes and add necessary rests.

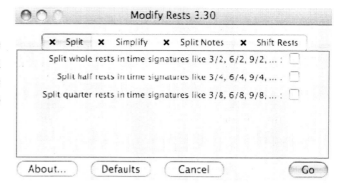

Easy Tremolos:

Converts all consecutive identical pitches into a tremolo. Plug-In options allow fine-tuning of tremolo notation, such as the number of beams.

Enter this:

to be automatically converted to this:

Create Cross Staff:

Automatically move notes from one staff to another where appropriate.

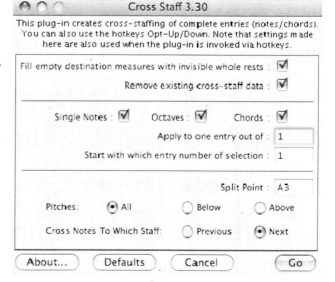

Smart Split Point:

Designed for use with piano music. Used to correct for split point errors (sections that you want to move notes to the other staff). It identifies notes which need to be moved automatically. To obtain the best result, you can help the Plug-in identify these notes by setting some options, such as the highest or lowest note that can occur in the bottom or top staff, etc.

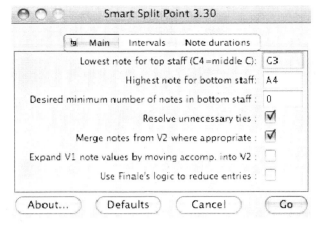

Process Extracted Parts:

This is the one Plug-in I personally cannot live without. The Process Extracted Parts Plug-in effortlessly separates chords, voice 1 and 2, and layers depending on which note you want to pull out. I find it indispensable in separating parts such as Horn I, II parts into separate parts as shown below.

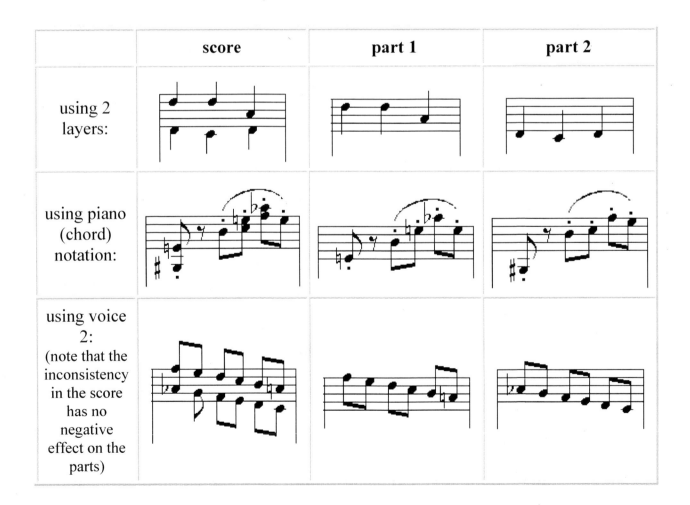

	score	part 1	part 2
using 2 layers:			
using piano (chord) notation:			
using voice 2: (note that the inconsistency in the score has no negative effect on the parts)			

<u>Smart Playback</u>:
Creates a playback effect for glissandi, hairpins, trills, and tremolos. Some musical items don't automatically play back in Finale. This Plug-In can prepare the following items for playback:

- Note-attached **glissandi** (via pitch-bend or fingered).

- **Hairpins**.

- **Trills** (requires articulation **or** smart shape trill: ).

- **Articulations, tremolos** and **percussion diddles**.

<u>Menu Shortcuts</u>:
Remaps keystrokes to menu commands.

 *I wholeheartedly recommend purchasing the entire set of TG Tools if you are going to do professional copying. You can access more information about them at **www.tgtools.de.***

Putting It All Together:

- Choose a few Plug-Ins you might find useful in the style of music you write.

- Take a look at the various TG Tools, especially Process Extracted Parts.

- Experiment with how these can help you work more quickly and efficiently.

Chapter 14
Customizing Finale

Finale Templates

Finale has several templates already defined for use. You can quickly start working on your music without having to set up your score manually or by using the Document Setup Wizard. To use a template, just click on "New From Template" under the file menu.

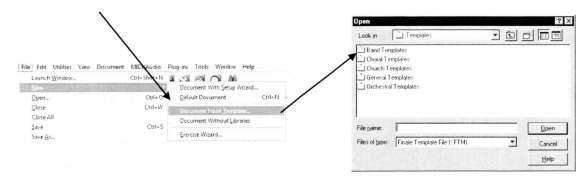

Bookmarks

Bookmarks are markers in your score to which you can quickly jump for easy editing and playback. These also can contain special settings about how to display the music.

To jump to a bookmark, click on its name in the bookmark menu.

Creating a Bookmark...

Click View→ Bookmarks→Add Bookmark...
- Name: what you want to call your bookmark.

- Assign to: Page View or Scroll View.

- Settings for Page View:
  - Page (the page to show in your score).
  - Scale View To (what zoom level you want to view on the screen).
  - Horizontal (moves your view to a specific horizontal position on the page).
  - Vertical (moves your view to a specific vertical position on the page).

- Settings for Scroll View:
  - Measure (the measure that you want to view)
  - Scale View to (what zoom level you want to view on the screen).
  - Staff Set (Chose a predefined Staff Set. See chapter 4 for more information on Staff Sets).
  - Staves (Position the view to show a specific staff on the top of screen).

Edit Bookmark…
Allows you to edit all the above options which you have previously created on Bookmarks. You can also delete Bookmarks by using "Edit Bookmark…"

Using Libraries

Finale's libraries contain reusable sets of musical elements such as articulations, expression markings, shapes, and chord-symbol suffixes. A basic set came with Finale-- they're in a folder called Libraries within your Finale folder. You add a library's contents to the active document by choosing **Load Library** from the File Menu. Feel free to modify these libraries, or to create new libraries containing your own sets of symbols.

To create your own library, choose **Save Library** from the file menu. Then choose what you want in your library from the 18 options (shown right). Finale will then export the settings from your file in the chosen category in a Library file, such as your set of Articulations or Text Expressions. Therefore, you can easily use markings and symbols from several files in the piece you are currently working to modify.
Some of the Libraries found in Finale are discussed below:

Articulation Shapes:
Contains shapes to be used for articulations. You can create shapes to be used as articulations using the Shape Designer.

Articulations (Maestro):
Contains a selection of single-character articulation marks that describe how a single note is to be played.

Chords & Fretboards:
These sets of predefined chord symbols are used by the Chord Tool.

Clefs:
Contains sixteen standard clefs.

Choral Dynamics:
Contains dynamic expressions set to Above Staff instead of Below Staff.

Default Fonts:
Contains the default font settings found in Document Options-Fonts.

Document Settings:
Holds all the settings saved within with your document such as the settings in the Document Options dialog box, plus a number of other settings in the Document Settings submenu, as well as other settings, such as the Playback Controls settings.

Engraver Articulations:
This library, similar to the Maestro Articulation Library, has a number of Engraver symbols to be used for articulations. These are already adjusted to take advantage of Finale's positioning settings.

Engraver Text Expressions:
This library contains text expressions using the Engraver Font. Expressions such as dynamics and tempo indications are included.

Executable Shapes:
This library contains six predefined Executable Shapes, which can serve as the playback definitions for expressions. (See chapter 10 for more information on using Executable Shapes).

Figured Bass:
Provides a simple starting place for entering figured bass in your document.

Fretboard Styles:
Contains four fretboard styles which define how Finale draws custom fretboard elements. The first three fretboard styles are the classic (4, 5, & 6 frets) style; the last was created with Jazz Font characters for a hand-produced look.

Harp Diagram:
This is a Shape Expression Library containing the two parts of a harp pedal diagram—the "skeleton" and the "pedals."

Instrument Libraries:
The General MIDI library is designed to work with most synthesizers' built-in sounds. Libraries are also included for the following synthesizers: Kawai K1, Korg M1, Proteus 1, Proteus 2, and Roland MT32. Each library contains a set of ready-to-assign Instruments (clarinet, piano, etc.) with the channel and patch numbers preset to match your particular synthesizer.

Jazz Articulations:
This is the articulation library to be used with the Jazz Font. It contains items such as staccatos, accents, house tops, falls, and glissandos.

Jazz Chords & Fretboards:
Jazz Chords Suffixes and Fretboards.

Jazz Clefs:
This library contains eighteen jazz clefs.

Jazz Default Fonts:
This library contains the default font settings for the Jazz font.

Jazz Document Settings:
Changes items in your Document Settings that are appropriate for use in the Jazz font, especially the alignment of notes with their corresponding stems and flags.

Jazz Dynamics:
This is a library containing text expressions for the Jazz Font.

Jazz Measure Rests:
This is a shape expression library which contains a multi-measure rest shape.

Jazz Page Format:
Contains default settings for the Page Format for Score and Page Format for Parts Dialog Boxes.

Jazz Rehearsal Letters:
Contains rehearsal letters from A-Z, all of which are enclosed in a box. This is also a text expression library.

Jazz Spacing:
Contains spacing widths for use with the Jazz Font.

Jazz Staff Styles:
Contains a basic selection of Jazz Staff Styles for use with the Staff Tool.

Jazz Stem Connections:
Contains stem connection definitions for use with the Jazz font.

Jazz Tempos:
Contains tempo indications in the Jazz font. This is also a text expression library.

Jazz Text Repeats:
This is a text repeat library for the Jazz Font. It contains items such as *D.S. al Coda,* etc. These expressions also come with brackets.

Measure Rest:
Contains the default Multi-Measure Rest symbol.

Page Format:
Contains default settings for the Page Format for Score and Page Format for Parts.

Percussion Maps:
Contains all the percussion maps you have created, as well as default percussion maps for General MIDI.

Pitch Bend:
This is a single Text Expression in a library by itself. It consists of the words "pitch bend," and has been defined to produce a single pitch bend. This pitch bend lasts for one whole note. It moves the pitch wheel from its "at rest" position all the way to the top of its range of movement, then back down to its "at rest" position.

Quarter Tone:
This Key Signature library contains a single key signature for a quarter-tone key system where there are three chromatic steps between two diatonic steps (instead of the usual one). If you set your piece in this key signature, bear in mind that one key on your MIDI keyboard corresponds to one chromatic step in the music. In other words, you won't be able to play normally and still get an accurate transcription of your playing, because—for example—the C# key on your MIDI keyboard will correspond to a C quarter sharp on the screen.

Shape Expressions:
Contains a selection of Shape Expressions for use with the Expression Tool.

Smart Lines:
Contains Smart Shapes available in the Smart Line Selection dialog box including glissandos, pedal indications, trills extensions, guitar markings, and other line-type markings that can be adjusted in the score.

SMS Markers:
Contains a collection of Text Expressions which are pre-defined for SmartMusic Studio Markers and can be added to the score to specify repeats, rehearsal marks, pauses, and other indications, while creating a file intended to be saved as a SmartMusic® Accompaniment.

Staff Styles:
This library contains a basic selection of Staff Styles for use with the Staff Tool.

Spacing Widths Libraries:

- Fibonacci Spacing.
- Fibonacci Edited Dots.
- Tight Spacing.
- Medium Spacing .
- Loose Spacing.

These libraries contain spacing width tables used for the spacing of notes and lyrics. Fibonacci Spacing is the default which spaces your music using a ratio of about 1 to 1.6. A quarter note will use 1.6 times the space of an eighth note.

Text Expressions (Maestro):

Contains a number of expression and dynamic markings, many of which have been defined for playback.

Text Repeats:

Contains a selection of text repeats—textual repeat indications, such as "D.S. al Coda," that are fully functional for playback.

Other Options:

Under the Edit and Document Menus are several sub-menus which allow you to specify how you would like to work in Finale. There is a plethora of options here that control the overall look and feel of Finale, plus settings for many other options. Check the Finale Users' Manual if you need more information on these options.

Below are some options under the Edit Menu. Please keep in mind that not all versions of Finale have all the same options or are set up in the same way.

Enharmonic Spelling:
Gives various options for key spellings in this submenu such as Default Spelling, Favor Sharps, Favor Flats, Use Spelling Tables (created by the user).

Measurement Units:
Allows you to choose from EVPUs, Inches, Centimeters, Points, Picas, or Spaces for the measurement system in the entire Finale program. (EVPU stands for ENIGMA Virtual Page Unit, of which there are 288 per inch.)

Program Options:
The Program Options dialog box lets you configure Finale's program-wide settings. For example, you can specify to save your preferences automatically when you exit Finale, or only when you explicitly use the Save Preferences command. The settings in this dialog box are saved in the Finale.INI file (in your Finale folder).

The following Program Options are discussed in detail. Note: not all versions of Finale have the same options or have the same screen layout.

New Options:

- **Default Document Name:** Type in the name of the Template you want to use for your default file.

- **Default New Operation-Setup Wizard/ Default Document:** Select one of these options to set the keyboard shortcut for New (CTRL/command-N) to the Default Document or Setup Wizard.

- **Startup Action: (**Document Setup Wizard/ New Default Document/New Document with Template/Open Document/No Action.) Select which item from the New submenu of the File Menu will be your preferred startup action.

- **Display Setup Wizard When Opening a Template:** Check this box to indicate that you would like to open the "Score Information" and "Score Settings" pages of the Setup Wizard to customize templates prior to opening them.

- **View Percent:** Percentage new documents should display when opened.

- **View: Scroll View • Page View • Studio View:** Select the view which new documents should display when opened. If Page View is selected, you also can select the Page View Style new that documents should use.

- **Maximize:** New documents are opened to a maximized window.

- **Show Rulers:** (Self Explanatory).

Open Options:

- **Open Older Documents As "Untitled":** Opens older files as "Untitled" instead of their original file name to protect you from inadvertently overwriting your older files, making them unreadable in an earlier version of Finale.

- **Require Confirmation After Conversion of Older Documents:** Warns when Finale is going to convert an older version file. You will need to click OK before proceeding.

- **Open Templates As "Untitled":** Templates are opened as an untitled document, requiring you to enter a name before it can be saved. This is done to protect you from inadvertently overwriting the template when you actually wish to save it as a new document.

- **Set Human playback for Finale Notation Files Created Prior to Finale 2004:** Choose this option to automatically enable Human Playback while opening files created in earlier Finale versions (pre-Finale 2004).

- **Automatically Convert Text In Files From Other Operating Systems:** Automatically converts to translate upper-ASCII characters (such as è, ö, and hard spaces) into the appropriate character on the current system. If Finale is unable to translate the character, it will display the problem character as a question mark. Finale will only check text fonts, as defined in the MacSymbolFonts.txt file, not music or symbol fonts. You can also show a dialog, after conversion about, the process.

- **Number of Recent Files In File Menu:** The number of files which appear in the list of recently used files in the File Menu.

- **Tie Conversion: PostScript/Screen/Ask When Converting:** These options are used when converting files previous to Finale 97 for determining how to handle ties.

Save Options:

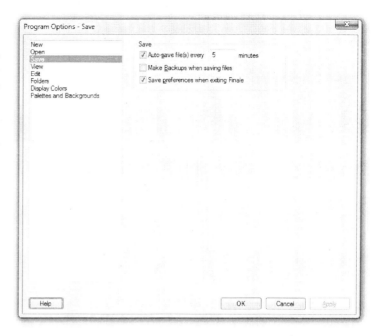

- **Auto Save File(s) Every ___ Minutes.** Finale updates a second copy (not the one you're working on) at regular intervals. This second copy of your file is stored in the folder specified on the Folders page of the Program Options dialog box discussed later in this chapter.

- **Make Backups When Saving Files.** Saves a backup copy of your file in the backup folder you specify in the Folders page of the Program Options discussed later in this chapter.

- **Save Preferences When Exiting Finale.** Automatically saves your preferences each time you exit the application. Turn this option off if you do not want Finale to automatically save your preferences.

View Options:

- **Show Tools Menu.**

- **Show All Messages:** Re-enables all messages you may have turned off with a "Don't Show This Again" checkbox.

- **Save Window States When Exiting Finale:** Saves the position of the palettes and windows when you exit Finale.

- **Load Window States When Starting Finale:** Loads the last saved position of the palettes and windows when you start Finale.

- **Custom Zoom 1 • Custom Zoom 2 • Custom Zoom 3:** Enter custom zoom percentages as you wish them to appear in the Zoom submenu of the View Menu.

- **Pitch Representation: MIDI Note Number • Pitch.** Choose how you want Finale to represent MIDI notes throughout the application.

- **Pitch Representation: Middle C = C3 • C4 • C5.**

- **Measure Numbers: Display Defined Measure Numbers • Display Actual Measure Numbers:** Select whether Finale will display the measure numbers that you defined in the Measure Number dialog box, or the actual measure numbers in the document.

- **Smart Hyphens and Word Extensions Update:** Allows you to turn off the automatic updating of hyphens and word extensions in the lyrics.

- **Hidden Object Shading:** Sets the shade percent age for hidden expressions (100% = hidden completely, 0% = no shading).

Edit Options:

- **Measurement Units:** Allows you to select the measurement unit you want Finale to understand—and display—in all of its dialog boxes.

- **Allow Undo:** Turning this option off will not allow you to Undo any previous actions, but may speed up other program operations such as copying or pasting a large section of music.

- **Allow Undo Past Save:** If this option is not selected, Finale will throw away your undo transactions after you save your file.

- **Maximum Undo Levels:** Sets the number of Undo levels to allow how far "back" you will be able to undo your edits. **Setting this option to 0 (zero will allow an unlimited number of undo levels.**

- **Music Spacing and Update Layout:** When dealing with how music should reflow when changes, such as adding or deleting measures, or changes to the size of a measure occur you have 4 options: 1) Do Not Reflow; 2) Reflow Measures: Only Within Systems; 3) Reflow Measures: Across Systems (Maintain System Locks); and 4) Reflow Measures: Across Systems (Remove System Locks).

- **Reflow Systems Across Pages:** This option determines whether Finale reflows staff systems into different pages.

- **Automatic Update Layout:** This option has no effect in Scroll View. In Page View, this option determines whether Finale will update the layout each time it redraws the screen.

- **Automatic Music Spacing:** Select this option to have your music automatically spaced as you enter it—at the end of a Speedy Entry measure, at the end of a HyperScribe session, or after each note in Simple Entry.

- **Use Fonts and Resolution from: Screen • Printer:** These options account for the differences between the screen and printer resolution. Choose Printer to ensure that the computations use printer fonts and resolution from the currently selected printer.

- **Arrow Keys Nudge Items by:** Enter a value to specify the number of pixels Finale should move a selected Special Tools element, such as a dot or an accidental, each time you press a nudge key.

- **Automatically Constrain Dragging:** To temporarily constrain dragging in the initial direction of your drag, press **shift**. If you prefer to have dragging automatically constrained, select this option.

- **Chime When Edit Complete:** (Self Explanatory).

- **Font Annotation:** Opens the Font Annotation Dialog Box, where you can fine-tune the selection area for font characters.

Folder Options:

This window allows you to specify the default locations for the following file types:

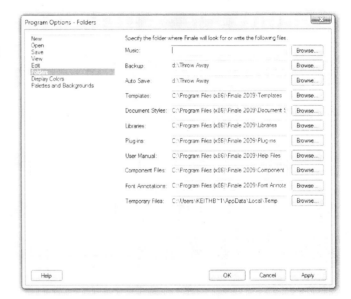

- **Music**

- **Backup**

- **Auto Save**

- **Templates**

- **Document Styles**

- **Libraries**

- **Plug-Ins**

- **User Manual**

- **Component Files**

- **Font Annotations**

- **Temporary Files**

Display Colors Options:

Allows you to assign colors to different layers as well as to different elements in your score such as Articulations, Text Blocks, and Smart Shapes. This is useful for differentiating between various objects in order to easily identify which tools created them, or to which layer they belong. Display colors can be printed. Select Print Display Colors in the Print dialog box. The color display settings are saved when Finale saves your preferences in the Finale.INI.

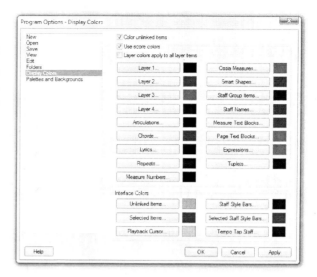

- **Color Unlinked Items:** With this box checked, items that have been broken in a linked part change color (to orange). The item in the score also changes color indicating that this item is broken into one or more parts. For example, if an expression is repositioned in a linked part, it will change color in the part indicating that future score edits to the positioning will not apply to that item in the part (see Linked Parts).

- **Use Score Colors:** Select this checkbox if you want Finale to display musical items in color. If it is not selected, color is not used for musical items, but is still used for the interface elements. To print using the display colors, this checkbox must be selected.

- **Layer Colors Apply to All Layer Items:** Select this checkbox if you want Finale to set all items in layers 1–4 to the specified colors for each layer, including items such as expressions, chords, and lyrics.

- **Musical Elements:** A number of items in your score can be assigned different colors. Click on any item button to choose a color for the item.

- **Interface Colors:** Some items in Finale appear only in the display to help you see how Finale is functioning behind the scenes. You can control the color of the interface items listed here. Click on any item button to choose a color for the item.

Palettes and Backgrounds Options:

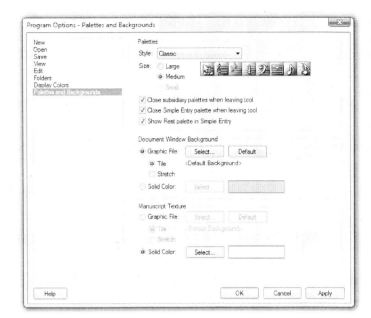

Allows you to customize the appearance of all Finale palettes as well as to customize the background color. You can change the size and style of all tool palettes and menu bars, as well as when you want them to appear based on the tool selected.

- **Size: Large • Medium • Small:** The small palette size will display the tool icons as they appeared in versions of Finale prior to Finale 2003.

- **Style:** Click this drop-down arrow to choose from a variety of styles for your tool palettes. The Traditional palette style is only available in the Small size.

- **Close Subsidiary Palettes When Leaving Tool:** Closes the Smart Shape Palette and Special Tools Palette when you change to another tool.

- **Close Simple Entry Palette When Leaving Tool:** (Self Explanatory).

- **Show Rest Palette for Simple Entry:** Shows the rest palette for Simple Entry.

- **Document Window Background: Graphic File/Solid Color:** Click the Select button when Graphic File is selected to choose one of Finale's backgrounds (or your own) to place behind the score as the background wallpaper. You can also choose a solid color.

- **Manuscript Texture: Graphic File/Solid Color:** Click the Select button when Graphic File is selected to choose one of Finale's manuscript paper backgrounds (or your own). You can also choose a solid color as your manuscript paper texture.

Document Menu Options:

There are a few Document Menu Options which we have not explored:

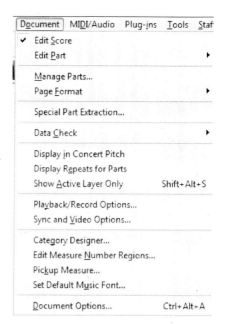

Data Check:
The Data Check submenu commands perform a variety of "housekeeping" tasks, mostly having to do with fonts and Finale's retention of deleted musical material. See Chapter 15 for more information.

Display in Concert Pitch:
See Chapter 4 about viewing your score transposed or in concert pitch.

Pickup Measure:
Sets a pickup measure at the beginning of the score. See Mirror Tool in Chapter 9 for creating pickups in the middle of a score and for those of different durations.

Playback/Record Options:
Specifies which MIDI data to record and/or to playback. See Chapter 10 for more details.

Sync and Video Options:
Controls how Finale handles MIDI Sync and SMPTE MTC synchronization with other devices and the movie window.

Document Options:
This menu provides the global settings for a variety of musical items such as barlines, augmentation dots, and ties. These options are fully discussed on the following pages.

Document Options

This menu contains Finale's strongest feature—full customization of every aspect of your printed music. Here you have complete control over every minute detail of your music from the position of dots and accidentals to the height and arc of a slur. In newer versions of Finale you can also load and save Libraries right from the Document Options window.

Following are brief descriptions of each setting. Note that not all options are in all versions of Finale. The options with a ✓ are particularly useful.

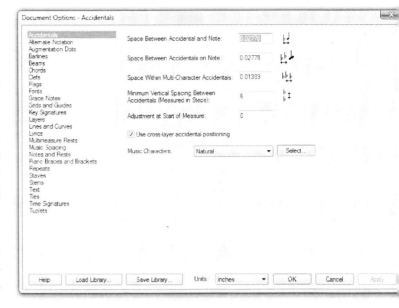

Accidentals:

Modifies the spacing of accidentals relative to notes and other accidentals. Also, changes the font character of any accidental.

Alternate Notation:

Customizes the spacing of alternate notation elements such as slashes and two bar repeats.

Augmentation Dot:

Sets up the global placement of dots on notes: adjusts the vertical placement, and specifies the distance between the notehead and the first dot, and the distance between dots on notes with two or more dots; moves the dot to the right for upstem flagged notes; determines whether to adjust the dots when it detects multiple voices.

✓ Barlines:

Fine-tunes the global appearance of Barlines in the score. Determines when to draw the left barline for staff systems, and whether it draws a closing (right) barline at the end of each staff system in Page View, or only at the end of the last staff system in the piece. Displays or hides all barlines in the piece.

With left barline turned off: With left barline turned on:

Beams:

Displays the Beaming dialog box where you can set a number of options relating to the angle, thickness, and style of beaming.

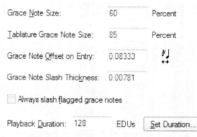

Chords:

Changes the font of chord items and adjusts their baselines.

Clefs:

Modifies the spacing of clefs and other attributes regarding clef changes and where to display clefs. Also includes Clef Designer where you can replace or edit any of the clefs - including their appearance, placement, and effect on the music.

Flags:

Makes global adjustments to flag positioning and spacing. Also, changes the font character of any flag.

Fonts:

Globally changes the font for many elements of your score. See Chapter 15 for more information.

Grace Notes:

Globally adjusts the spacing of grace notes, as well as modifies sizing and playback attributes.

Grids and Guides:

Displays the Grid/Guide options where you can set various options related to the display and actions of grids and guides.

Key Signatures:

Controls where to display key signatures as well as adjusts their spacing.

*Old key signature **is** cancelled at key change.*

*Old key signature **is not** cancelled at key change.*

✓ **Layers:**

Allows you to choose automatic stem direction, tie direction, and rest placement settings for each layer. You can also choose if the layer will playback or if the music spacing is affected.

Lines and Curves:

Modifies thickness of various types of lines, and specifies curve resolution.

Lyrics:

Adjusts syllable positioning for lyrics, as well as settings for hyphens and word extensions.

✓ **Multi-Measure Rests:**

Specifies options for multi-measure rest settings. You can choose to use the standard multi-measure rest shape or an alternate style of notation for multi-measure rests. The symbolic style combines whole and double-whole rests to represent block rests of different lengths, commonly those of eight or less measures.

Standard Multi-Measure Rest: "Old-Style" Multi-Measure Rest:

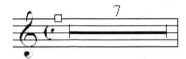   

✓ **Music Spacing:**

Gives you options for music spacing such as minimum measure width, collision avoidance settings, and spacing library specifications.

Notes and Rests:

Specifies note shapes for durations, adjusts music spacing relative to barlines, shifts rest positioning, and selects new font characters for notes and rests.

Example:

Piano Braces and Brackets:

Options controlling the change of thickness, shape, and curvature of the curly brace that brackets piano staves.

Regular look piano brace

"Modified" piano brace

Repeats:

Specifies line thickness, line and dot spacing, and various other options.

Regular looking repeat   *"Modified" repeats*

Staves:

Settings for controlling staves in documents used as Document Styles.

Stems:

Controls the length and thickness of stems. Also, creates or edits stem connections for custom noteheads in your score.

Normal Stem Length:	0.25167	♩↕
Shortened Stem Length:	0.20833	♩↕
Half-Stem Length:	0.0625	♫↕
Reverse Stem Adjust:	0.75	↳↕
Stem Line Thickness:	0.01215	
Stem Offset for Noteheads:	0.01389	
☑ Display reverse stemming		
☑ Use stem connections	Stem Connections...	

Text:

Controls various parameters relating to entering text and text inserts. **Remember:** the other text inserts (title, copyright, composer, etc.) are found under the File → File Info menu.

Ties:
Changes the global definition of ties.

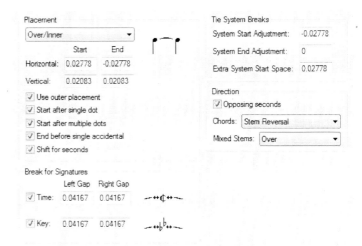

✓ Time Signature:

Globally changes the font size, style, and spacing of time signatures. Used also for turning off the symbol abbreviation **C** for 4/4 and or **¢** for 2/2 (see below).

Abbreviated 4/4 and 2/2

Non-abbreviated 4/4 and 2/2

Tuplets:
Changes the global definition of tuplets.

Customizing Palettes (PC)

In newer PC versions of Finale, you can now totally customize all the tool bars by adding/removing tools and by reorganizing the layout of the tools. To change the layout of a toolbar, select Customize Palette under the Window Menu. Then select one of the tool palettes that you wish to customize.

You can then add or remove specific toolbar buttons and rearrange them by moving them up or down on the palette. If you want to revert back to the default layout, click "Reset."

Tool Sets (Mac)

In Mac versions of Finale, you change the layout of tools by using Tool Sets. Shift-drag the tool icons on the tool palettes to swap their locations. There are four combinations of tool sets to use (Master Tool Set and Tool Set 1, 2, and 3). To save the layout of the tools you have created as one of the three Tool Sets, hold down OPTION and select Program Toolset 1, 2, or 3 from under the View menu. To switch from one palette setup to another, choose its name from the Select Tool Set submenu.

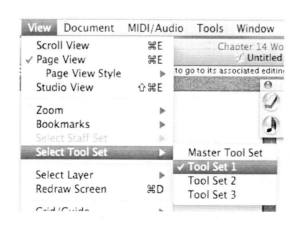

Chapter 15
Advanced Finale Topics

Tools covered in this chapter are listed below:

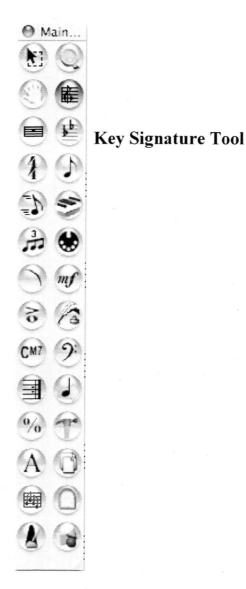

Key Signature Tool

Merging Scores with Score Merger

Finale's Score Merger allows you to combine several files into one. This can be done horizontally, with files appended after each other, such as different movements of a symphony or a collection of songs. Or, it can be done vertically, consolidating individual parts into a full conductor's score.

The Score Merger function is found under the File menu. First, add the Finale files that you want to merge then arrange them in the correct order with the Move Up and Move Down button.

Merge Into One File Options:

- Choose this option if you would like to merge scores horizontally, one file after another as you would in movements of a score.

- Append to Current Document
    - Insert at Current Selection.

- Treat as Independent Movements
    - Insert Blank Pages to Maintain Left/Right Layout. (Treats each merged file as a separate movement. Finale will adjust the page breaks and final bars for you automatically.)

- Keep Each File's Measure Numbering.

- Edit Instrument Junction between Files. If checked, the Instrument Junction dialog box appears for each file, which allows you to edit the proposed instrument linkage.

Merge These Parts Into One Score Options:

- Check this box to merge scores "vertically" in order to, for example, combine a collection of part documents into a full conductor's score.

- Adjust Systems to Fit Page- Automatically adjusts systems to fit page after merging vertically.

General Merge Score Options:

- Optimize MIDI Channels: Adjusts for duplicates in the GM MIDI channel and instrument setup.

- Generate Report • View Last Report: Logs any errors that occur while merging files. Click View Last Report to view Score Merger's most recently generated report.

Non-Standard Key Signatures

In addition to the standard major and minor key signatures, Finale allows you to create keys that deviate from the circle of fifths. To create your own key signature, choose "Nonstandard" from the Major/Minor dropdown menu in the Key Signature tool.

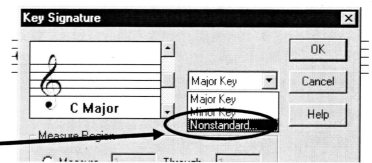

Linear Key Format:

Linear Key format allows you to add more than the traditional 7 sharps or flats. Use the scroll box to add more sharps or flats as shown.

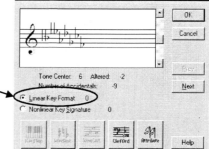

Nonlinear Key Signature:

If you want to completely abandon the circle of fifths, the Nonlinear Key Signature allows you to choose which accidentals to display.

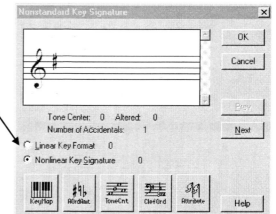

AordAmt (Accidental Order and Amount)-
Use this to specify which note will be sharp or flat.
The "Step Levels" correspond as follows:

C	0
D	1
E	2
F	3
G	4
A	5
B	6

Sharp = 1   Double Sharp = 2   Etc.
Flat   = -1   Double Flat   = -2   Etc.

Example: To make D sharp and an A flat, set Step Level 1
to "1" and Step Level 5 to "-1".

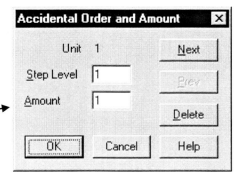

You can see that the flat on the A was placed above the staff.
You must use the ClefOrd (Accidental Octave Placement) button to
specify on which octave the accidentals will be placed:

Unit: The position number of the accidental in the
        Key signature that you created. In this example
        Unit 1 is the D-sharp and Unit 2 in the A-flat.

Octave: Middle C = 0

        C above Middle C= 1
        C below Middle C= -1

Clef: The ID of the clef. **(Accidental
        placement must be defined
        separately for each clef.)**

        Treble = 0   Alto = 1
        Tenor = 2   Bass = 3

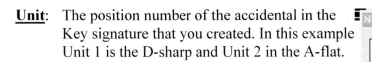

Other Options:

Key Step Map:
Use this dialog box to specify octave structure for a nonstandard key signature.

Tone Center:
Use this dialog box to specify the relationship between the number of accidentals in a nonstandard key signature and the tone center of the key.

Attributes:
Use this dialog box to specify the following special attributes for nonstandard key signatures:

- **Harmonic Reference:** Sets the fundamental root tone (0 = C). This is rarely changed.
- **Middle Key Number:** Sets the MIDI key number that corresponds to the Harmonic Reference number you've indicated (Middle C = 60).
- **Symbol Font:** Changes the font for accidentals or enters the ID number of the font.
- **Symbol List ID:** Changes the symbols used to represent sharps, flats, and so on, or enters the ID number for the Symbol List you want to use.
- **Go to Key Unit:** Sets the number of scale steps between each pair of keys on your MIDI keyboard. For example: In a quarter-tone scale, there are 2 steps between scale steps; Key Unit = 2.

Delete:
Used to revert to settings used for the standard major scale.

Exercise 15.1
Try to create the following key signature:

Hints:
- You may have to delete any other alterations that come up by default when you first create your key signature.
- Add an alteration of +1 to the F step level.
- Add an alteration of -1 to the B step level.
- Lower the B-flat in the treble clef one octave.
- Lower the B-flat in the bass clef one octave.

Creating Your Own Clefs- Clef Designer
The Clef Designer can now be found under the Document Options/Clefs.

Finale supplies sixteen standard default clefs for use in your pieces (see right). You can modify these clefs or replace them with custom clefs, using new symbols if you prefer (you can either use a symbol from a font, or design a new graphic clef symbol yourself).

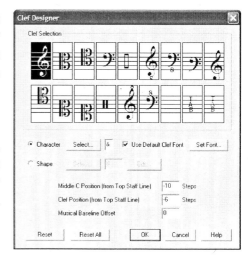

If you define a new clef, Finale will treat it intelligently, correctly renotating any music that follows it and always keeping track of the playback pitches of the notes. Any new clefs created appear in the standard palette of sixteen clefs (replacing existing clefs).

Clef icons- These icons illustrate the sixteen clefs defined for this piece. Click an icon to select it for editing.

Character: The character you enter in the symbol text box tells Finale what symbol to use to represent the clef when it appears in the score. The symbol always appears in this text box in the system font, even if you've specified a different font for the actual display. For example, the treble clef appears in this text box as an ampersand (&), even though in the score (and in Finale's music font) it looks like the G-clef symbol (&).

If you're not sure which letter corresponds to the symbol you want to use, click Select. Finale will display a palette containing every available character.

Shape: Select/Edit- Click Shape to create a clef based on a shape. Creating a shape is the same as creating one by using the expression tool except a staff background is shown to help draw the shape.

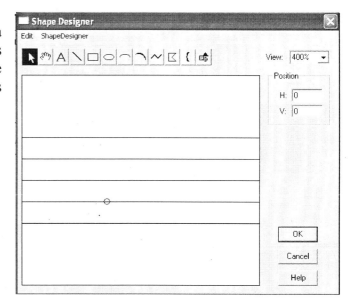

Middle C Position (from Top Staff Line, in steps) - The number in this text box specifies the middle-C line for this clef. A value of zero places middle C on the top line of the staff. The actual value in this text box indicates the number of lines and spaces middle C is to be from the top line. For example, the treble clef, which places middle C one ledger line below the staff, has a Clef Adjustment value of –10 because one ledger line below the staff is ten lines and spaces below the top line of the staff. Note that when you move the position of middle C, the key signature will move with it.

Clef Position (from Top Staff Line, in steps) - This value, measured in lines and spaces from the top line of the staff, determines where the new clef will sit on the staff. A value of zero places the baseline of the clef on the top line of the staff. Note that the baseline of a clef isn't quite the same as the baseline for regular text; the baseline of a clef is determined by its musical meaning. For example, the baseline of the treble clef isn't the bottom of the character—it is the "curl" that's centered on the G line of the staff. The baseline of the bass clef is centered between the two dots (the F line), and so on. Thus, the Clef Position for the treble clef is –6-- six lines and spaces lower than the top line of the staff.

Musical Baseline Offset- The value in this text box sets the distance between the normal baseline for each clef (as defined in the previous item) and its vertical position when it occurs as a clef change (and hence at a reduced size). It is measured in the currently selected units which are inches by default.

Clefs in the Maestro, Petrucci, Engraver, Jazz, and Sonata music fonts are automatically positioned correctly when they occur as clef changes, but symbols in fonts you design yourself may require this extra adjustment.

Reset/Reset All- Click Reset to return the selected clef to the default clef in a Coda font (Petrucci, Engraver, Jazz, or Maestro). Click Reset All to return all the clefs to the defaults.

Other Hints:
- Save your Clefs as a Library and import them into any document (see Chapter 13).
- You can import graphics into your shape when you create it using the Shape Designer (see Chapter 3).

Exercise 14.2
Try to create the clef below or your own unique clef.

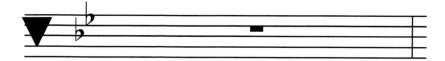

More on Selecting Fonts

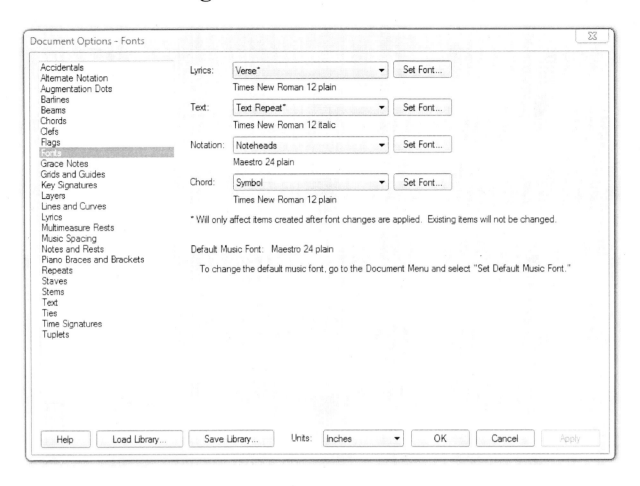

This dialog box lets you change the font for almost every element in your score from lyrics, to text, to any musical symbol.

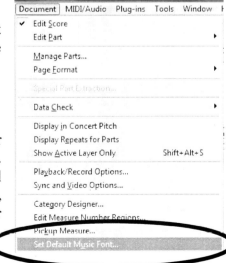

If you want to change the default music font, you can do that separately by selecting "Set Default Music Font..." under the Document menu.

Maestro, a music font provided with Finale, is the default font for the musical symbol elements such as Music, Clef, Key, and Time. However, Finale offers you the option of setting these musical elements in any other music font, such as Engraver, Jazz, Petrucci, Sonata, or Crescendo. You can mix and match fonts to suit your taste.

Data Check Options

Also under the Document menu is the Data Check sub-menu. Several "housekeeping" functions are there to help you deal with missing fonts, permanently remove deleted items, and make sure your Finale file is in perfect health.

Font Utilities...

This dialog box tells Finale to inspect the font of every musical element in your piece—articulations, expression marks, chord symbols, the music itself—in search of the font you've specified, and replace each occurrence of it with another font you specify. This is particularly useful if, for example, you decide you want to change the font for all your tempo markings at once, or all your chord symbol suffixes.

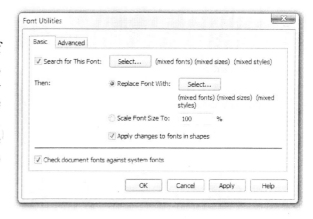

Check Document Fonts Against System Fonts:
Choose this menu item to compare the font list in the file opened to the font list of the computer being used.

The Advanced tab has more options related to font management dealing with fonts in files opened cross-platform.

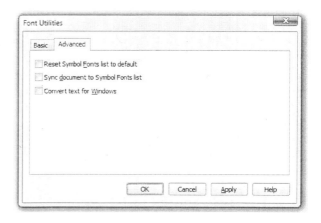

- **Reset Symbol Fonts List to Default:** Choose this option to restore the default list of Symbol Fonts in MacSymbolFonts.txt.

- **Sync Document to Symbol Fonts List:** If a document is saved on a Macintosh, where a font such as Times is listed as a Symbol Font, then opened on a Windows computer where Times is NOT listed as a symbol font, this command updates the document to treat Times as a non-Symbol Font.

- **Convert Text for Windows:** This command tells Finale to convert higher ASCII text font characters (such as è, ö, and hard spaces) to the appropriate font encoding for Windows.

File Maintenance

This command performs a variety of "housekeeping" tasks, mostly having to do with fonts and Finale's retention of deleted musical material. In previous versions of Finale, this command dramatically reduced the size of your file. In newer versions (since 2004), much of its housekeeping tasks happen automatically behind the scenes.

This also allows you to remove duplicate library elements in Text Expressions, Shape Expressions, and Articulation.

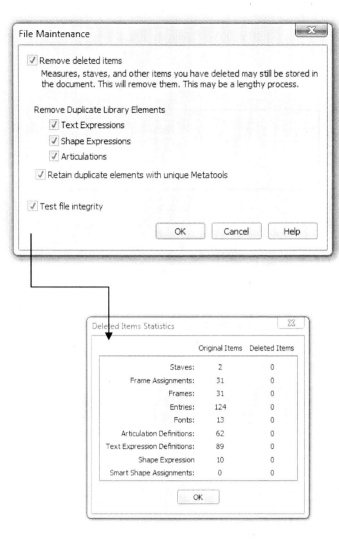

Test File Integrity

This command performs a check to verify the integrity of your file. It will alert you to any problems it finds such as missing music or where problems might have occurred. If you use this command religiously, you will rarely have any problems with file corruption. It gives you a sense of well-being that at least Finale considers your file to be okay. (This is a PC only command on some earlier versions of Finale).

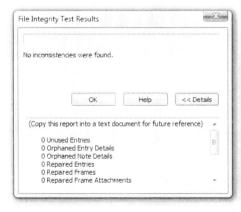

MicNotator®

If you have a microphone connected to your computer, you can use it with MicNotator as an input instead of using a MIDI keyboard.

MicNotator is found under the MIDI/Audio menu, under the Device Setup submenu.

- To use MicNotator, click the **Enable MicNotator** checkbox.

- Set the MIDI Recording Channel or simply leave it on 1.

- Make sure have the proper sound input source selected for your computer.

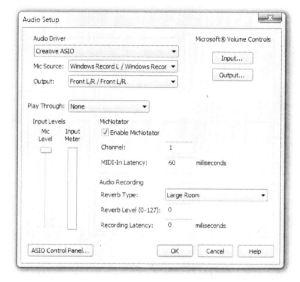

- Sing or play some notes. Check your input level with the little graph and adjust the Mic level as needed. As with recording, levels too loud will cause distortion and MicNotator will function improperly. Levels that are too soft won't be picked up at all.

- Click OK, and you will be ready to use MicNotator in Speedy Entry, Simple Entry, or HyperScribe. It's a good idea to use the Caps lock method of entry for Speedy Entry so you can play with both hands and not worry about entering the durational values.

- For more information about recommended Mic placement, consult the Finale Users Guide.

Importing from Other Programs

Other than its own native files, Finale can open and convert files from the music notation programs shown here.

To open the following file types, go to the File Menu and chose "Import:"

File type	Versions
Encore	3.0 through 4.2.1
Rhapsody	1.0 files
Score	all
MIDISCAN	2.5
SmartScore	1.3.1

Keep in mind that the more complex the file you are importing, the more likely you will need to do some editing after the conversion process. See the Finale Users Guide for more detailed explanations for importing each file type and known issues and how to solve them.

Using Finale between PC's and Mac's

Finale has always made it easy to use its files cross-platform. Put your Finale file on a disk that is readable by both platforms and Finale will be able to open it. In very early versions of Finale you needed to use the ETF (ENIGMA Transportable File) format. This is no longer necessary. Finale flawlessly reads and writes to both Mac and PC versions. If going from a Mac to PC, it is best to use a PC disk since Macs can usually read and write to PC disks. The reverse is not the case unless you have a special utility installed which allows you to read Mac disks on your PC.

When upgrading your Finale files to more recent versions, Finale will convert the file to the newer version when you open it as an "untitled" document. This allows you to save the converted file with a new name while keeping the older version untouched. While Finale can always open and convert from old versions, it still lacks the functionality of saving a file in an older version. For example, Finale 2009 can open Finale 2001 files without any problem. However, once the 2001 file is saved with Finale 2009, it will no longer be readable by Finale 2001. You might want to consider using the free Finale NotePad to view or print any files that you have converted.

SmartMusic Accompaniment®

SmartMusic Studio® is an interactive, computer-based practice program for woodwind, brass, string, and vocal musicians, also published by MakeMusic!

In newer versions of Finale, you can export your Finale score as a SmartMusic Accompaniment. To do so, choose "Export SmartMusic Accompaniment" under the File menu. After selecting a few options regarding how you want to set up your accompaniment file, your file will be saved as a SmartMusic Accompaniment file which can be opened in SmartMusic Studio.

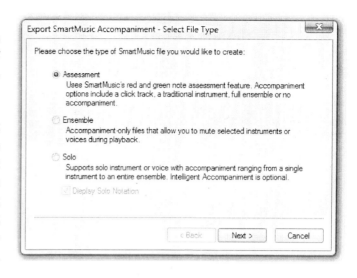

There is more detailed information in the Finale Users Guide regarding preparation of your score for SmartMusic Studio.

MusicXML

In Finale 2006, we saw the demise of ETF (Enigma Transportable Files) which were used in very early versions of Finale to move between Mac and PC. Any version from 2006 to the current can now export a Finale document as XML. MusicXML files can be opened in other music programs as well as in earlier versions of Finale.

Finale can export MusicXML 2.0 files, MusicXML 1.1 files (for use with Finale 2006 and 2007), as well as MusicXML 1.0 files (for use with Finale 2003 to 2005 on Windows).

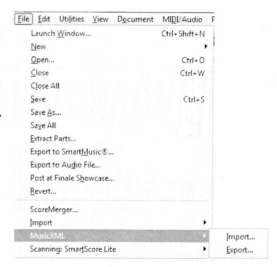

Scanning

To speed note entry, try scanning your music into Finale. You can import scanned files from Musitek's MIDISCAN or SmartScore software. Or, you could directly open the scanned files in Finale, using the new SmartScore technology (which has replaced the MIDISCAN feature of previous Finale versions).

Some limitations of SmartScore Lite:
- No articulation marks, hairpins, double or repeat barlines, or text scanned.
- Will only do 3 accidental types (sharp, flat, double sharp).
- 3 clefs (Treble, Bass, and Alto).
- 16 staves per page.
- Smallest note value is a 32nd note.
- Maximum of 1 augmentation dot.

A few tips to remember when you are scanning your music:
- The clearer and cleaner the original, the better the scan. Stray marks and smudges adversely affect accuracy.
- Use grayscale <u>not</u> color.
- Save your scan files as TIFF.
- Higher resolutions do not always produce better accuracy. Try 300 dpi to start.
- Try increasing contrast by 25% if you are not getting good results.

How to use SmartScore Lite:

- You can either scan and import your music while in Finale.

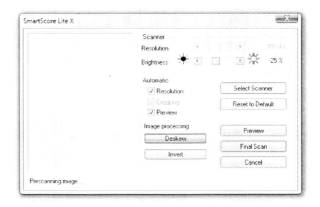

- Or, you can import existing TIFF files.

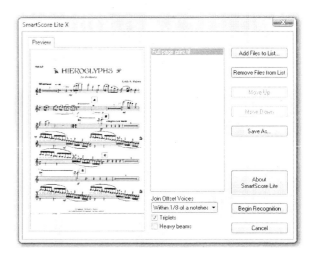

- Both these options are selected under the File Menu → Scanning: SmartScore Lite.

- If you are scanning within Finale, just follow the prompts to scan and import all your pages.

- If you are importing existing TIFF files, click "Add files to list..." and browse to the TIFF file(s) on your storage drive.

- When finished adding files, click "Begin Recognition".

- Proofread your music and make any necessary edits or corrections.

Some things to check after your music is scanned and converted:
- Slurs and ties.
- Key signatures in files with more than one staff.

Other SmartScore Lite options:

Join Offset Voices: Never...Within 3/4 of a notehead:
This is the amount of space between noteheads of notes that occur at the same time. Usually occurs on seconds where the note heads are offset slightly so that you can see both clearly. If you have notes in voices that are not being converted properly, try increasing this value.

Using Finale on the Internet- Finale Reader

The ability to post your music on Finale Showcase is back, and easier than ever. Choose Post at Finale Showcase... from under the File menu to get started. Your music can then be viewed online with the free Finale Reader.

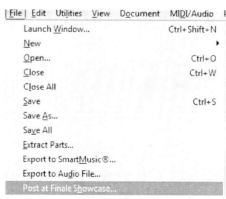

With the release of Finale Reader, Finale NotePad is now no longer free and is a $9.95 download or a $19.95 CD purchase. So we have come full circle and are back to the Finale Reader which can open, play, and print Finale family notation files and MusicXML files.

About the author...

Keith with the original box from Finale version 1.0.

A native of Pittsburgh Pennsylvania, Keith Bajura received his BFA. in music composition from Carnegie Mellon University. His teachers have included Roland Leich, Leonardo Balada, Lucas Foss, George Tsontakis, Nancy Galbraith, and Marilyn Taft Thomas. Professional orchestras as well as high school orchestras have performed his music locally in Pittsburgh. Two of his compositions *Hieroglyphs for Orchestra* and *An Evening in Transylvania* were specifically commissioned and premiered by the Bethel Park and McKeesport High School Orchestras respectively to much acclaim.

At Carnegie Mellon University, Mr. Bajura taught several music technology courses covering topics ranging from music sequencing to digital sound production and manipulation and, of course, Finale. He has done work as a professional music copyist using *Finale* for the Pittsburgh Symphony, Pittsburgh Opera, Pittsburgh Ballet, and the River City Brass Band as well as for several world-renowned composers.

Mr. Bajura has produced two stress-relieving CD's entitled "Relaxation for the Soul" which blend environmental sounds with traditional melodies. Using only computer generated material, he paints a musical background with electronic oceans, flowing water, and bird calls, fused with more traditional classical and inspirational themes.

He has been active in church sacred music for a number of years as both organist and choir director at several area churches.

In addition to those in music, Keith Bajura has held positions as Director of Technology for both the School of Music at Carnegie Mellon University and West Mifflin Area School District. He is currently Director of Technology at Aptech Computer Systems Inc. in Pittsburgh, Pennsylvania.

INDEX

E

F

G

H

I

K

Q

R

S